FACE TO FACE

*Gay and Lesbian Clergy on Holiness
and Life Together*

Jeffrey Heskins

scm press

British Library Cataloguing in Publication data

A catalogue record for this book is available
from the British Library

0 334 04003 5

First published in 2005 by SCM Press
9–17 St Albans Place, London N1 0NX

www.scm-canterburypress.co.uk

SCM Press is a division of
SCM-Canterbury Press Ltd

Typeset in Albertina by Regent Typesetting
Printed and bound in Great Britain by
William Clowes Ltd, Beccles, Suffolk

Contents

To the members of the Clergy Consultation

Introduction

The Church is no stranger to controversy. The most casual of glances at its history confirms this, and I have no real problem with that in itself, as disagreement and controversy are often signs of life and growth. But what has always been a dilemma is the manner in which it tries to resolve those disputes and remain faithful to the call of Christ. Matters of common faith, holy living and an understanding of the nature of God have often been the subjects on which the Church has debated at its lively best, but the zealousness adopted by some of those doing the debating has often left an unfortunate trail of havoc and destruction that is its worst.

At the beginning of the fifth century the Church was gripped by one such bitter dispute. Augustine, Bishop of Hippo in North Africa, locked theological horns with Pelagius, a British lay monk who had travelled to Rome and become an influential teacher and spiritual director. Pelagius taught that human beings were themselves responsible for good or evil deeds and attacked Augustine's doctrine that humans were born in a state of sin because of the sin of Adam and that they passed this sin on through the procreation of each new generation. Augustine in turn accused Pelagius of reducing the Christian faith to a set of moral rules and declared him a dangerous heretic. The followers of each man became increasingly vitriolic in their publications and denouncements, until any notion of discerning God through listening and careful discussion was lost. Winning the debate and silencing the other became their ultimate objective.

This was finally achieved in the year 418 when Augustine successfully lobbied for a council of bishops to be convened. The Council of Carthage met under Pope Zosimus and pronounced Pelagius a heretic and excommunicated him. Thus silenced, Pelagius is said to have died alone in Palestine a few years later. Nearly all of his work was lost or destroyed and history (always written by the winners) accords the blame for this controversy to him rather than his adversary, the winner, Augustine.

Perhaps the greatest tragedy of this episode of history is that it would appear that the two men never met. They fought for years in theological debate but never saw or heard each other face to face. Would the outcome have been any different if they had? Of course we can have no idea, but I wonder if the blame culture and pursuit of winners and losers might have been replaced by some more worthy insight?

Human sexuality, and in particular homosexuality, has been the issue that has lit the touchpaper for the Church in the late twentieth century and the beginning of the twenty-first. The rhetoric has often been vitriolic, moving away from informed discussion and careful listening. A lot of ink has been spilled in researching and writing and there are some who consider the subject to have received far too much attention in the pecking order of important matters.

The accusation that is often made of Augustine is that he was more concerned with power and controlling the Church. This is a charge that has been levelled at different interest groups within the contemporary Church. Some have been defined as religious extremists seeking to overturn a once benign and inclusive institution only to redefine it in their own narrow and destructive image.[1] If that is so then it has become a Church that needs rescuing from itself. What this book sets out to do is to steal back the essence of the debate by refusing to play the game of winners and losers and by inviting more voices into the conversation to challenge the bullying and theology done by threat.

It does not pretend to be a conversation exploring the different sides of the various arguments and perspectives around the subject of gay and lesbian relationships and whether they can be accommodated or tolerated within the Church local and universal. I make no apology for that. Instead what it aims to do is two-fold in principle. First, it gives space to the voices and experience of those gay and lesbian lives that the primates and bishops of the 1998 Lambeth Conference said they wanted to listen to – and we all might benefit from that listening experience. To that end I hope that this book will go some way to re-balancing what many perceive as an unevenly balanced discussion. Second, it looks at what it means to do that kind of listening. Are we simply listening to voices somewhere out there in the theological ether of academic polemic? Or are we listening to the voices that are prompted and provoked within each of us when reflecting properly on what this whole discussion of same-sex love does to each of us? Any book on sexuality issues is bound to ask the reader questions about what it means to live as human beings. This is not just about them – it is about all of us, and what it means to live alongside each other. Furthermore, in that process of listening and reflection it invites the participants in this book to do their own reflecting. How can any gay man or lesbian woman, ordained or lay, live a life of holiness in a faithful partnership that remains outside the official support of the Church? What does it mean to try?

If you are a reader who has hitherto felt excluded from sharing your view, or hasn't really known what all the fuss was about, or is simply fed up with all the rancour and posturing, this might be a helpful way into a discussion that has been dominated by the pressure groups and those using remote theological language. If you simply want your already established views confirmed, you really should go and buy another book. This one does not purport to have the final say in the matter, but I hope it will contribute something to our understanding of whatever God is in the process of revealing to the Church in our day.

I find myself writing this in the week that the Windsor Report is published.[2] There has been little time to digest its suggestions and implications for the Anglican Communion and beyond, but already, before the ink has barely dried, the usual voices have announced themselves with breathtaking speed to the world's press for fairly predictable comment. Have they really learned nothing about human listening and the need to take time to absorb what the other is saying? Whatever the merits or failings of the report put together by Archbishop Eames's working party, it has the wisdom in its final chapter to commit itself and all of us to an ongoing dialogue of measured speech and careful listening.[3] It is likewise important not to declare this book to be any kind of final word, for Christians who believe in revealed truth should remember that revelation takes time to be recognized and to be seen.[4] The Windsor Report also finds itself published on the feast of St Luke the Evangelist and Physician. Perhaps in the search for healing and commitment to the gospel we might discover that in measured speaking and careful listening we might find ourselves

> ... holding together people of very different religious views so that they belong together in order that they might come to some sort of agreement rather than having to agree in order to belong.[5]

Whether or not Windsor does that, I hope that for some this book might enable the first steps towards engaging in a topic that has frozen much of the Church with the fear of engaging at all, by bringing you almost face to face with some of those who have had to live through it all. If it does that, it might put us all back in touch with the search for perfect love and why we need it so much.

Jeffrey Heskins
St Lukestide 2004

Notes

1 Richard Holloway: jacket comments, Stephen Bates, *A Church at War*, I. B. Taurus, 2004.
2 The Windsor Report: The Lambeth Commission on Communion. Web site: www.anglicancommunion.org/windsor2004.
3 The Windsor Report, conclusions.
4 David Jenkins, *The Calling of a Cuckoo*, Continuum, 2003, p. 171.
5 Professor Timothy Jenkins, Dean of Jesus College Cambridge, speaking on the *Today* programme, 18 October 2004.

Who do you think you are?

ASKING THE AWKWARD QUESTION

Begin at the beginning and go to the end and there stop... It sounds simple enough but what was the beginning? Haven't you ever wondered about where things start?[1]

Begin at the beginning and go to the end. This has always seemed to me to be the common sense thing to do, but in truth, in this instance, the more I have thought about it, the less obvious the starting point. I have begun writing this book twice now and as I sit at my desk, thinking about the things that have disturbed the Church of England and the wider Anglican Communion since the summer of 2003, I am more and more baffled by my Church's inability to enter into any meaningful dialogue on matters concerning human sexuality generally, and the rather more thorny subject of gay and lesbian relationships in particular and especially those that relate to the clergy.

Three events have followed hard on the heels of each other this summer. The Diocese of New Westminster in the Canadian Province decided to make authorized provision for same-sex couples to be blessed in church. A voluntary service of covenanted union was drawn up for those parishes applying to make use of the rite, and at the end of May Michael Kalmuk and Kelly Montfort were the first to make use of it at a church in East Vancouver. Within a few weeks the Episcopal Church of the United States of America had elected its first openly gay man to the vacant see of New Hampshire. Canon Gene Robinson, though not the first gay man to be made a bishop, was the first who lived openly with a partner of the same sex in a faithful relationship. Before anyone in the Anglican Communion had time to draw breath again, the Church of England, the Mother Church of the Anglican Communion, had, through its own unusual processes of selection and nomination to the Episcopate, announced that Canon Jeffrey John, also an openly gay man, living in a faithful but celibate partnership of many years, was to be the next Bishop of Reading in the Diocese of Oxford. The three events combined to produce a vintage of silly season summer madness. By the end of it, despite being given royal assent, John was forced to withdraw his acceptance in what appears to have been a brisk and unexpected meeting at Lambeth Palace, Robinson was under armed guard, having received death threats and been advised not to travel, and the emerging strong arm of the communion, most notably in parts of the African continent, were declaring themselves out of communion with New Westminster. Where in all of that does one begin any kind of sensible and creative reflection?

I suppose that none of them constitutes a starting point for me. They are important and their very existence as historic events need further attention and reflection. What I want to do, however, is to begin with an experience that happened to me, more than 20 years ago.

It is an episode that I clearly remember as if it were only a week ago. A hot summer afternoon at the beginning of June saw me making my way to keep an appointment with the bishop who was to ordain me. I had just finished my theological training at a residential college, which had not been the easiest of experiences, and I was looking forward to cutting my teeth on parish ministry. Since my early teens I had wanted to be a priest and here I was on the threshold of the dream. The bishop was a very easy man to be in the company of. I felt relaxed as we talked about the training that I had completed, the parish I was going to and what my hopes and aspirations were for ordained ministry. We drank a lot of tea and he allowed me to ask him all the questions I wanted. Then there was a slight pause in the proceedings before he cleared his throat and told me that there was something that he needed to ask me. He then began by apologizing to me for having to ask it, and before I could grasp the fullness of the situation he had uttered the words, 'Do you prefer men or women?' It was a split second that seemed like a full minute before I realized that, as I was single, he was asking me a whole gamut of questions, about my sexual orientation, whom I found sexually attractive, how I might react to sexual attraction, perhaps even what I might choose to do about it should it be an occurrence in the parish. It was another split second before I responded. He was visibly relieved that I gave him an answer at all and that I did it with good humour and courtesy. He made an embarrassing riposte and we moved on to the next thing that he needed to discuss with me. At the end of the interview, he agreed to ordain me to my title parish.

As my bishop I liked him very much. However, I remember feeling at the time that I had sold out to a principle that should have seen me armed with sufficient courage to tell him to mind his own business. I was irritated with him for asking and annoyed with myself for so readily supplying the answer. Since then, I have had occasion to think about the moment with a good deal of sadness, particularly when other clergy friends of mine tell of similar experiences when they are interviewed for new posts in the Church. It was the wrong question to ask and he asked it badly.

It was an abusive question. He was in a position of power. I wanted to be ordained and it was within his capacity as bishop to offer ordination and a job, with a stipend and a home for the next three years. It was what I had given up my life to train for. All of that was on the line.

It was an intrusive question. He was asking me a question about my inner life that, in itself, would have no real bearing upon my ability to perform my duties and ministerial responsibilities as an ordained minister in the Church. It is a question that, in this form, could not have been asked by an employer of a potential employee anywhere else without infringing basic human rights.

It was a destructive question, or it could have been had I not given the easy answer and enabled us to move on. But he had me cornered. What if I had lied to him for a quiet life? What if I had stalled him, or simply refused to answer? How would that have laid the foundations for a pastoral relationship between a senior pastor of the Church and one who was just about to launch off into the unknown territory of parish ministry? If I were to be loyal to him and my oath of canonical obedience have some meaning, all of this would have been in jeopardy.

It was an awkward question and one that he felt awkward in asking, but it has become clear to me over the years since then that it was
not really *his* question. It has rather become for me the sign of a
neurotic obsession of an institution that has a wholly inadequate
mechanism for dealing with matters of sexuality and relationships.
The Body of Christ has a real sense of awkwardness when dealing
with issues of the body. In one sense the bishop's question was quite
simply the wrong question. Had it been one about the manner in
which I conducted my relationships, that would have been a fair
question, and one with some pastoral concern. It would have been
enormously helpful too. As a single curate I had great difficulty
adjusting to the implications of what it meant to have any kind of
private life within a public ministry. Just how far was I the property
of the congregation (as some clearly think their paid ministers are)?
What did one do about personal relationships in the public domain?
Was it all right to be tactile with someone you loved, in the parish, out
of the parish, behind the closed door of the curate's flat, which was
not your own but went with the job, or anywhere?

Had it been a question that he asked to *all* his prospective new
curates it would at least have been fair in the sense of being the wrong
question put to everyone. But it was not. It was designed to extract the
awful truth as to whether I was gay or not. That in turn might have led
to the next question of whether I was celibate or not, and that might
have led to a discussion on how I should conduct myself in a manner
befitting a member of the clergy of the Church of England. Had I been
married, I am sure it would all have been very different!

Of course, the answer I gave him was that I was straight. His awkward riposte was then that it was the Cub mistress that I would have to
watch out for. We laughed it off: that was the easiest thing to do and
we had given ourselves the easy way out, but there was something
important to be learned from the encounter. The awkward questions
of who we are as sexual human beings, how human sexuality informs
and influences just who we are, and how we can be effective ministers
because of rather than in spite of it, will not be laughed off for ever. It
is precisely those in the Church who spend so much time telling us
that there are more important things to be concerning ourselves with

as a Church and a communion, who are the very people who have never experienced being shunned, sidelined, rejected or passed over for preferment (the nice word for promotion) because they are gay or lesbian. For this very reason we should continue to give time and energy to this matter; for unless we can sort out and deal with the matters of human relationships and what that means alongside each other in communion, we have little hope of speaking with a voice that sounds authentic in our drive for God's justice and the values of God's Kingdom in the wider world.

So in pursuit of a way of answering the awkward question, where do we go next? Ironically, I propose to go to the Lambeth Conference of 1998. For those gay and lesbian supporters of the Church the conference confirmed all the misery they felt of being excluded. For the world's press it was a scoop. For the bishops of the Anglican Communion it was a public relations disaster. Yet even there, in a university on a hill overlooking the Mother Church of the Communion, there was the tiniest of silver linings to the storm clouds.

Lambeth 1998 and the Report on Human Sexuality 2002

The Lambeth Conference of 1998 drew together most of the bishops of the Anglican Communion. As such it is a conference that meets every ten years to discuss and listen to various issues of concern across the communion. A report was prepared prior to the conference under the title *Called to Full Humanity*, under the leadership of the Archbishop of Cape Town. The report included a section on human sexuality, and the bishop's working party had included a number of gay and lesbian participants. I attended the part of the conference when this section was to be discussed, as a guest, like many others taking time away from work to do so, and was appalled to learn that at the last minute the long-standing invitation to gay and lesbian clergy to give a presentation was withdrawn. The signs were there on the first day when I attended the press conference. A reporter who at first sight seemed to be reasonably intelligent asked that if the Church was to listen to gays and lesbians should it not also lend a sympathetic ear to bestialists and paedophiles? Worse was to come. Offering the same reasons, a significant pressure group of bishops indicated that they would walk out of the debating hall if the presentation by a small group of gay and lesbian clergy took place.

After a long debate on a hot summer's day, in an atmosphere that one bishop later described as what he imagined a Nuremberg rally to be like, the conference made a series of recommendations compounding the sense of exclusion that many gay men and lesbian women already felt. These included an unwillingness to sanction or legitimize the union of same-gender couples and to withhold ordination from such people in active relationships. Both of these had been features of the House of Bishops of the Church of England report *Issues in Human Sexuality*,[2] published seven years previously. The voting was overwhelming. Of the 739 bishops at the conference, 526 voted in favour, 70 against and 45 abstained; 98 bishops chose not to attend the debate at all, preferring instead to go on a day trip to France, which I suppose is a different form of denial and another way of not dealing with the awkward question at all.

One of the brighter elements of the recommendations to emerge from the debating hall that day was that the bishops made a commitment to listen to the experiences of gay men and lesbian women. Following the conference the then Archbishop of Canterbury, Dr George Carey, set up a working party of archbishops and bishops with a remit to explore the divisions among Anglicans over sexuality.

By August 2002, the 'international conversation' of 12 bishops and primates had met three times and produced a response called *Report on Human Sexuality*.[3] The outcome of the report was that the 12 had 'not been able to reach a common mind regarding a single pattern for holy living for homosexual people'. While nothing was resolved in essence, there were good signs that at least the dialogue had deepened and that the working party had learned to be respectful of each other's differences. The report mapped out a careful process that the primates and bishops had agreed, in which they would listen respectfully to each other and commit themselves to pray together. One of the most crucial insights they gained was that they dealt better with each other when they met face to face, something that Jim Cotter picked up on in an appraisal he later made of this report:

I must admit that my spirits rose on reading that 12 Anglican bishops and archbishops met over a long weekend for each of three years to listen to one another's views on sexuality in general and homosexuality in particular. Perhaps something good had come out of this Nazareth. And in some measure that is true. The report on their meetings is refreshingly different in its approach.[4]

Cotter's reaction was far more generous than my own when I read the document for the first time. It didn't seem to say anything new or radically different and I suppose that my impatience was not really met by the gentle tones in which it was couched. But I think Cotter was right in suggesting that something new was indeed happening, for it was in the simplest of insights that the primates and bishops were able to convey that perhaps a way forward was offered.

We have committed ourselves to the hard work of seeking to be open to one another, listening in a spirit of hospitality and charity. We believe that respect for our Communion is fostered when we as bishops engage in face-to-face conversation across provincial lines. We encourage the development of similar conversations between other lay and ordained provincial leadership around issues vital to our common life. This discipline of seeking the truth and speaking the truth is especially important when information flows freely around the world due to contemporary technology. Our experience has re-affirmed our conviction regarding the importance of face-to-face communication. No amount of e-mail can take the place of it.[5]

It was hardly rocket science, but I suspect, given the vehemence of their disagreement in 1998, it was an important discovery: one small step for the bishops, one huge leap for bishop-kind, and something we can all learn from. I see it as critical to our approach to the whole issue under discussion; so much so that it forms the title of this book. What has been missing from the whole process from Lambeth 1998 has been that dimension of the face-to-face encounter. Despite making the pledge to listen to the gay and lesbian experience, few seem to have taken that pledge seriously, giving rise to the increasing suspicion that it is simply not going to happen.

> Talk of 'listening' to gays and lesbians is little more than a condescension to be jettisoned when no longer convenient.[6]

It is in an attempt to confront that suspicion and to begin a record of that experience that this book devotes its attention. For how can we answer the questions of meaning and purpose if we do not give some attention to the experience from the perspective of those who are gay men and lesbian women?

The primates and bishops didn't know what to recommend to gay and lesbian couples seeking to live a holy life, but did anyone ask what gay and lesbian couples already do to seek patterns of Christian holiness? What does it mean to live a 'holy life'? Should the pattern for 'holy living' be any different for gay and lesbian couples than for anyone else? Is it possible to answer these questions in an abstract and theoretical way? Where do all the gay and lesbian clergy stand now in the wake of these proposals? These are some of the areas that will fall under investigation as we invite gay and lesbian clergy first to tell their stories and reflect on them and second to share some of the everyday experiences of living as clergy in partnership with another of the same sex. This is not simply an exercise in voicing opinions. I hope that it will be a deepening of the listening exercise that we have barely begun, and will serve to inform an ongoing local, national and international process of reflection and discussion.

Richard and Tom

In her book *Memories of Bliss*, Jo Ind[7] reminds us that our bodies are very complex and that it is probably a mistake to see them simply as physical entities. They are always changing because they are always in process. Whether we choose to call it ageing or dying or maturing or growing, our bodies reflect the experiences that we have in life. She goes on to tell us that such experiences impact upon the body in different ways, and to illustrate the point she tells the story of her favourite theologian, a Brazilian called Rubem Alves, speaking to a group of students in Maine, USA. During the lecture he and a student took a bite of an apple. Alves made the point that although they both ate from the same apple and they both liked apples, it would mean different things to each of them. He had grown up in a country where apples were not readily available. As a child he believed they were magic fruit because he only knew of them through the story of Snow White. When his father first brought him an apple after a trip away, Alves did not dare to eat it. Instead he looked at it and polished it, and to this day when he eats an apple it puts him in touch with this childhood memory. So the body is a container of stories and experiences, all of which make up the person who is the teller of those stories. In that sense it is both descriptive and a mystery of memory waiting to be unlocked and perhaps show us a new way of seeing things. We might perhaps recognize for the first time that the assumption we made when thinking about our bodies, feelings, sexual identity, attractions and a whole host of other things that we experience, while possibly being the same (I cut my finger and experience pain – and so do you), will be different because of the associations it might have and the memories it will evoke (I remember falling from a tree and cutting my finger as I grabbed a branch, but yours was cut while you were tortured in prison for your political activism).

> But the body . . . is also a container of memory and the holder of dreams. It is changed and is changing through habit and practice. The body is the site of thought. It is the means through which we think and is itself changed through thinking. When I say we are turned on through the body, I mean we are turned on through memories, experiences, habits and words – words that are written in our flesh.[8]

Richard and Tom have a story. It is written in their flesh. To some it is the story of a couple of poofs, queers, benders or botty boys. To the Church for much of the time it is a story belonging to 'practising homosexuals' and one that until recently has remained unheard and unwanted. For Richard and Tom it is a story that describes survival in the face of hostility, companionship in loneliness, support in crisis and encouragement to succeed. They have lived together for 25 years and can remember the exact date they met. Introduced by mutual friends at a New Year's party, they immediately knew there was something about each other that connected. Richard worked for an insurance company in town and Tom had just finished his Post Graduate Certificate in Education and was about to start a job as a secondary school teacher.

Richard had known as a teenager that he had feelings for other men. He liked their company and he found them attractive, but it bothered him because as a devout and committed Roman Catholic he knew that his Church considered such feelings to be vile and sinful. He had told his school chaplain at the age of 17. The priest was a good man and had counselled him that young men of his age often entertained feelings like these in their teens, that it was a passing phase and he would grow out of it. He never did. He was an only child, born late to parents who had long thought that they were unable to have children. His arrival had been greeted with joy and seen as a gift from God. They had doted on him, brought him up to be faithful in his Mass-going habits and seen him well educated at Catholic boarding school. He loved his parents and had a good relationship with them, but had been unable to tell them his greatest and most terrible secret. The prospect of shaming them within the Church and disappointing them by not delivering the hoped-for grandchildren was a phenomenal burden and one which grew into a loneliness that was unimaginable. At Durham University he was something of a solitary figure, though not without friends entirely. He sang in the college chapel choir, where he met Peter, whom he thought would change his life. In a sense he did, but not for the better. Peter was bright and attractive, but like a lot of young students he was still unresolved as to who he was and what he wanted. What Richard had thought might be love turned out to be a mere predatory attempt at sex. It was a frightening experience and one that made him retreat faster and further into himself.

In his final year he shared a house with two women, which is how he met Sheila. She was a Catholic and they had a lot of interests in common. They both liked to read and walk in the countryside. For the first time he found a fondness and friendship that made him feel safe. Sheila fell in love with him. They married. It was a disaster. He knew from the first days that it had been a mistake, but somehow the idea of marriage made him think that he could change his sexual identity. Sheila was devoted to him and he did love her. They would be companionable in old age. Children were unforthcoming and although his parents were delighted that he had married a lovely Catholic girl, the questions about when they might start a family became a pressure as he faced not only his parents but his wife too. The feelings of attraction to other men did not diminish either, as he had hoped they might. Eventually he resolved to tell Sheila. Upon breaking the news to her everything changed. She became anxious and suspicious if he was out late at night, and although he remained faithful to her he knew that she was worried. He would often find her crying when he came home. After much heart-searching they resolved to separate. Richard changed jobs and moved away in an attempt to start life over again. It was a lonely time, and the lowest point of his life.

Tom, by contrast, had been brought up in a fairly lively family espousing liberal, 'laissez-faire' values. His mother was a committed Anglican Christian who took him along to the local parish church, which he liked. It was very traditional and high – a product of the nineteenth-century Tractarian movement. The music, light and colour appealed to him and although most of his friends were unsympathetic and not inclined to join him as he grew into his teens, he saw it as part of the cultivated eccentricity that he tried to develop for himself. He did church – they didn't. What commended it most was the vicar, who got him involved in things and who made him think about who he was and what he wanted for himself. The vicar was a man who was not afraid to ask questions and ruffle feathers. He spoke boldly on issues like nuclear disarmament, racial discrimination (particularly apartheid in South Africa) and the inadequacies of the social policies of the government of the day.

Tom also knew that he had particular feelings for men. Although he didn't dislike women, he never had any sexual feelings for them as he grew up, and just assumed that it was the same for everyone else.

One day he would wake up and it would all be different. Then he would have grown up. Until then he felt it part of the spirit of the age that he should go on a voyage of personal discovery. It was a way of life he had not heard denounced from the pulpit of his local church and it was a freedom that most of his peers seemed to enjoy. Tom was a bright young man, but disinclined to adapt himself to study at school. He failed his A levels and took some time off to travel and think, which his parents supported financially. Tom travelled in the United States, and one summer he worked as an assistant at one of the many youth programmes that American churches participate in during those months. That was where he met Jim.

Jim had been brought up in a fairly enclosed Christian community in Oklahoma. The community was tightly knit and run strictly by the elders who constantly monitored the membership. Any lapses in attendance at worship, or perceived lapses in personal moral stand-ards, were met with severe retribution in the form of public humili-ation or expulsion. Jim was gay. When word got out about this, he was reprimanded, humiliated before the congregation and finally 'cast into outer darkness', as the rescinding of his membership was described. He had to leave town. He moved to the north, where he joined a congregation of the United Church of Christ, who openly welcomed him. Tom was quite struck by this, since he had never come across a Christian denomination that would reject him on the grounds of who he was. Later, when he got to know more about the Church, he came to see that the issue was not so much who he was, as whether or not he expressed it.

He returned to England and told his parents that he was gay. His mother was enormously supportive and understanding. His father was not. There was no outburst of anger or rejection; it was simply a conversation that his father never wanted to visit. It created an atmos-phere they both tried to live with for a while, but Tom knew that the time was fast approaching to move permanently from the family home. He was offered a university place in Durham to read theology, and went and threw himself into a new life, in a new place with new friends. It was here that he met Richard who had returned to a place of familiarity after his marriage collapsed.

Tom read for his degree without great enthusiasm and upon graduating decided that he might make good use of his life by teaching. So he stayed on at Durham to study for his PGCE. That year he had decided to stay up over the Christmas and New Year holiday and had been invited to a party. Richard was there too. They each describe it as a moment of significant change. They got on well, and at the end of the party Richard offered Tom a lift home and they agreed to meet the following week. They fumbled their way through an awkward first few weeks of what might be classically described as 'courtship', and found a fulfilment in each other that was indescribable. Richard began to heal from the wounding he had felt and the guilt of what he had unwittingly done to Sheila. Tom, the reluctant student, found someone who cajoled him through that final year. By the summer they had agreed to live together and have been together ever since. That was 25 years ago.

Much of that time has been lived out in a social context of acceptance and affirmation. Their friends were warm and loving in their support and always saw them and treated them as a couple. Their local church was the same. There were a number of gay couples where they worshipped but other members of the congregation just got on with it. If one of them was absent from worship, the church members would ask after them. Everything was fine until Tom decided to pursue a calling to ordination. In this experience he saw the worst face of the Church's dual standards.

Richard, though he had been a faithful companion in Tom's life for what was by then 15 years, didn't feature anywhere in the process for selection. The Director of Ordinands recommended that Tom be cautious in speaking openly about Richard, advising that while he himself was supportive, the bishop would not be. Both men found it uncomfortable living openly in a world which by and large accepted them, but wanting to serve a Church that was at best undecided about them, and in which their relationship had to remain, for many, a secret. Tom would have liked to be ordained as a full-time paid employee of the Church, but decided to remain in teaching. He and Richard would continue to live together in the house that Richard had bought, which kept them less visible as a couple and therefore less of a 'risk' to the authorities of the Church they were preparing to serve.

Richard was now retired, and was able to support Tom who taught school by day and became a student himself in the evenings on his regional ordination course. He typed up Tom's essays for him, tracked down and borrowed books for him and did as much as he could to help. The course director and staff were supportive of both men and Richard was invited to the occasional weekends that husbands, wives or partners were encouraged to participate in. However, mid-way through the training course the director retired and a new one was appointed. A significant change ensued. The following year, at a weekend for 'spouses', as it had now become, Richard arrived to be told that it was not appropriate for him to be there. The wife of one of the new student intake had made a vociferous complaint regarding his attendance and had threatened to make waves. The new director asked him to leave and his supportive participation in this aspect of the course was disallowed.

It was a moment of unkindness in what was otherwise a happy and exhilarating training programme. The student body were openly supportive and rallied round in the face of Richard's exclusion. Tom went on to ordination. His bishop didn't ask the awkward question and Tom went back to serve the church that he and Richard had come to worship in. They are still there.

For Tom and Richard, the publication in 1991 of the House of Bishops' statement *Issues in Human Sexuality* compounded the general sense of confusion that pervaded the Church over gay and lesbian partnerships. The section that suggested that such faithful partnerships were a blessing to many but could only be entered into by lay people was a highlight of this confusion.[9] They were one such couple. They had been living together for 15 years before the report's publication and Tom was now already ordained. What were they supposed to do – disappear? By 1998 and the Lambeth Conference this sense of confusion had reached epidemic proportions. But there were signs that the epidemic might be treatable. The resolution passed at the end of the debate declared that the conference 'could not advise the legitimizing or blessing of those in same-sex unions, or ordaining of those

involved in such unions'. However, it went on to declare its commitment to listening to the experiences of gay and lesbian people.
Perhaps in so doing, the bishops of the conference established a theological homeopathic remedy to what they perceived as the ills of the
Church. Homeopathy is the remedying of like with like. So, if the
Church (or a significant part of the Church) has problems with gay
and lesbian partnerships, what they seem to be saying is let's apply
the experience of some of those partnerships to what we already
think we know about gay and lesbian couples and see if it moves our
thinking to a different place. This seems a very sensible thing to do. It
is what this book is about.

Method and structure

A sample of couples volunteered to take part in the research for this
book. In some cases both partners are ordained, but in most only one
partner is in holy orders. Some are training for ordination and might
well be ordained by the time this book is available for wider reading.
About a third of the couples are women. The social context of the
couples is varied. From County Durham to the Sussex coast, they are
drawn from a variety of settings. Many live in urban areas but others
live in town suburbs and a few in rural communities. Some were very
open to their names being disclosed while others were not. For the
sake of consistency, no names have been used.

All couples took part in tape-recorded interviews, each lasting
about one-and-a-half hours, which were then transcribed and re-
viewed by the couples for alteration and addition. Since this is a book
intending to give the opportunity to hear their experiences and
inform the wider discussion, these interviews will be quoted from
extensively.

I am indebted to the couples who agreed to meet and open up their
lives to a complete stranger. It is the finest form of hospitality that one
human being can offer to another, not only to open your home, but
also to share the home that is your life with another. I am grateful for
their trust and hope that I have been faithful to them in the reflections
made and insights offered. Without their courage in speaking out we

would not have that taste of the experience of gay and lesbian life that the Lambeth bishops and primates pledged themselves to listen to, and we would doubtless continue to wade through the quagmire of rhetoric and posturing that has long dogged this issue.

The next chapter concerns itself with the whole process of what we call reflection and reflective practice, which is academic-speak for how individuals, local church groups and the wider Church engage in the process of thinking about what they are doing: what is happening to them, how they are seen and what effect that has on them. I have included it because it seems to me that this is what the entire exercise concerns itself with. How do we engage in the business of listening to the experiences of others and taking account of how those experiences and their tellers affect us? It is what each of the couples was asked to do. Reflection or reflective practice is something that most of us, when pressed, might agree is a good thing to do, but will either do badly or not at all. However, if the reader wishes to pass over this chapter and go straight to the stories and reflections, it is quite possible to do so without spoiling the effect.

Notes

1 C. Day Lewis, *The Otterbury Incident*, Heinemann Educational Division, 1950, p. 1.
2 The House of Bishops of the General Synod of the Church of England, *Issues in Human Sexuality*, Church House Publishing, 1991.
3 *Report on Human Sexuality*, Forward Movement Publications, 2002.
4 Jim Cotter, 'Trying Ever So Hard', in *Lesbian and Gay Christians*, Winter 2002, p. 10.
5 *Report on Human Sexuality*.
6 Steven Shakespeare, *Church Times* letters, 31 October 2003.
7 Jo Ind, *Memories of Bliss*, SCM Press, 2003.
8 *Memories of Bliss*, p. 47.
9 *Issues in Human Sexuality*, 5:17, p. 45.

We had the experience but missed the meaning[1]

REFLECTIVE PRACTICE —WHAT DO YOU THINK YOU ARE DOING?

In 1996 I began a series of conversations with members of my church congregation in south London to discover what they thought about gay and lesbian couples in committed relationships and whether or not such relationships could be sustained within the life of the Church. The process took two or three years to complete and the result was a published book.[2] The purpose of the exercise was quite a simple one. It was to offer everyday people in one particular church community the chance to join a discussion that had hitherto been monopolized by the Church's theological elite. It was theological discussion done in a different way. Through a series of day conferences, small discussion groups and individual interviews, regular members of the congregation were able to record their thoughts and feelings about gay and lesbian couples who approached the Church requesting services of blessing and affirmation for their relationships. We wrote up the process and its findings and then shared some theological insights and pastoral images in wider discussion with the grass roots of the Church. The findings and the practical suggestions for welcoming gay and lesbian couples to the church were published in 2001.

Essentially reflective

Unheard Voices describes a ministry that had begun in 1978 and continues to this day. It is a part of the regular roundabout of pastoral care that our local church has offered to the local community for 25 years, and sits alongside those of marriage, baptisms, funerals and the other day-to-day pastoral needs of people in the locality. It was a different contribution to the discussion because it was a local one, involving people who would never otherwise get into print. For us as a church community it was an important exercise, because it gave us the chance to reflect at length on something that had been, for many, an infamous part of our past. Not everyone had supported the initiative to offer services of blessing for faithful gay and lesbian couples, and there were still some dissenting voices, but somehow they had hung in there together despite their differences. What was it that had enabled this? To find out, I remember suggesting, in an issue of the parish magazine, the idea of reflecting on pastoral practice. The following month I read this reply to the editor from a long-serving member of the church.

> There must be many new people at St Luke's, including possibly the Rector who will be unaware of past deliberations by the PCC and others on many contentious subjects . . . He gives the impression that there has been no theological framework to pastoral practices re homosexuality at St Luke's. It was as if he was negating all that has gone before . . . Of course, past practices must be scrutinized and possibly altered in the light of new ideas . . . but please do not make the mistake of thinking that this hot potato has not been the subject of prayerful, informed thinking and debate in the past.[3]

Quite right, and I told the author so. However, reflective practice is not the same as thinking about what you are going to do, though it may well have some influence on what we decide happens next. If we want to discover what contribution an individual or a group have made in any discipline of life, we need to see what has changed, or what new insight has been gained that was not there before. What we learned as a local church was that the issue that had the rest of the Anglican Communion tearing at each other's throats, was, when met face-to-face in the lives of real people, not nearly as bad as it had been in our imaginations. Listening to the lives of gay and lesbian clergy will, I hope, prove a similar point to those prepared to listen.

During the exercise, the participants were often surprised at how much their own thinking and attitudes had changed over the years. Many were able to admit that members of their own families were gay or lesbian. They described how glad they were that the social climate had changed sufficiently for their relationships to be openly acknowledged within their families. Some even took them as role models for family living.

> I know some people (within my own family) who are in long-standing partnerships. Some of them are the most responsible adults I know. If my children grew up to be as good and responsible as they are, then I would be happy.

> My sister is a lesbian and she has been living with this partner for years and they bought a house and so on and it is much like any other marriage really.[4]

In a similar fashion, following the publication of *Unheard Voices* a number of letters arrived. The correspondents declared relief at the chance to listen to the voices of regular people recounting their experiences and describing the effect on their thinking. A pensioner told the story of a gay cousin who committed suicide by swimming out to sea and drowning because his parents 'couldn't take it'; a Lutheran pastor said that it had made him look again at inclusive ministry within his church in Germany; an Anglican bishop, though disagreeing with some of the findings, was appreciative of the process and presentation. Finally, a retired Anglican priest, who was grateful that it was not the product of a single voice but of a community struggling with difference, wrote:

> The fact that you have carried your congregation along with you is a wonderful example of 'Christopraxis' and just shows that when Christian love is explained in truly Jesus-terms most people are led to re-consider about how it works in everyday life. So, well done all of you.

Consultation with the Consultation

What finally brought this book about for me was not the international events surrounding the proposal to consecrate the first openly gay man in a partnership as a bishop, but a day spent with the Clergy Consultation. The 'Consultation', as it calls itself, is a gathering for gay and lesbian clergy, whether celibate or partnered, and exists to offer support and encouragement for gay and lesbian clergy in the United Kingdom. It is an opportunity quite literally to 'consult' with one another on issues that are pertinent to gay and lesbian clergy or ordinands in training. It is not a secret society, but its membership is held confidentially precisely because the climate within the Church at large is at best changeable and at worst hostile towards them. This is not simply a perception held by a few nervous gay men and lesbian women, but a living reality for many of the company assembled.

I was invited as a guest speaker in 2002 to offer some reflections on affirming gay and lesbian partnerships in the local parish church with services of blessing and prayer. It was an unforgettable day, as I sat before a sea of faces reading a précis of one chapter of the book my church had put together. That this group had to exist at all seemed to me a contradiction of all that it meant to live as the Church. Yet here they were, a hundred men and women, all of whom had felt the calling of God to serve as priests in a Church that seemed to spend much of its time questioning the authenticity of their existence and the integrity of their lifestyles. What did the Church really know about them? And why, with such a prevailing culture of negativity, did so many gifted gay and lesbian priests choose to stay within that Church? These are awkward questions, but they are not impertinent if we are to discover something of the aspiring to a holy life in a same-sex household, whether parishioners and church members really are scandalized if the vicar is gay and lives openly with a partner, or whether any of this inhibits the priest's ability to be 'wholesome examples and patterns to the flock of Christ', as the Bishops' report *Issues in Human Sexuality* puts it.[5]

It is these members of the Clergy Consultation who have volunteered the stories and insights that make up the chapters which now follow. I am profoundly grateful to those who volunteered to share their life stories and life secrets, and to spend time with me reflecting on what it means to be gay, ordained and being in a partnership with someone of the same sex.

Establishing a process

Finding an appropriate way of reflecting is not as easy as it might seem. While reflective practice is something of a buzz-word in the world of Practical Theology, if you ask people what they really mean by it or how they go about it, you will get a variety of responses. A couple of years ago in a series of meetings with students in training for ordination I asked them to tell me what they understood by it. One group said that it was part of their course, a checklist of things that they had to do: a list of experiences to be had and a box to tick against each of them when the task was done. This seemed to me to be anything but reflective practice.

Elsewhere, a couple of students said that they were encouraged to keep a journal in which they were to reflect on their experiences while on their course and particularly their training experiences while on practical placements. This seemed more promising. So I asked how they set about making use of the reflection exercise. They didn't. The journal-keeping was entirely voluntary and secret. No one else ever got to know the contents of the journal, or even asked whether it was being kept up. There was no dialogue or sharing of insights at all. This seemed a rather pointless exercise, going through the motions of doing the reflection but then making no use of it to challenge perceptions, enhance insight and self-awareness or to offer ideas for improved practice.

Finally I came across one newly ordained curate who had astounded her post-ordination training group by announcing that her vicar, at regular intervals, took her for coffee and asked her to reflect with him on each new aspect of ministry she had experienced. He made her think about how she had felt at the time of the pastoral encounter and compare that with her feelings in hindsight. They talked about whether it gave her any new insights into herself as a person and a priest and whether it offered her new insights into what she thought she knew of God. She said she found it all quite useful because it not only made her think about what she was doing, but helped her see how she came across to other people.

For the most part, if we value the idea of reflective practice in ministerial training, then it is clear that most clergy and ministers don't know how to go about it, or can't find the time for it, or think that it is something else. This does not bode well for an exercise in which we are about to commit ourselves to listening to the experiences of gay and lesbian clergy in partnerships. However, there has been some useful thinking done on the matter from within the world of scholarship. Practical and Pastoral Theology purports to take the whole phenomenon of human experience seriously because it sees 'the essence of *praxis* as both action *and* reflection in pursuit of God's truth'.[6] Of all the methodologies suggested, the one I have found the least complex and most useful to adapt is offered in an article written by the British practical theologian Stephen Pattison, 'Some Straw for the Bricks: A Basic Introduction to Theological Reflection'.[7] In it he recognizes that some of the more abstract theories of pastoral theologians didn't really help those wanting to develop reflective practice to get started. So he suggests a model of 'critical conversation'. This is a simple way of trying to address the complex relationship between the experience gained from the situation and the theological and other ideas and theories. He suggests that anyone wanting to engage in some sort of theological reflection done in a creative way can do so by adopting a three-way dialogue or conversation style that comprises their own perceptions, feelings and beliefs, those belonging to Church tradition and those of the contemporary situation under scrutiny. That is what I propose to do here.

Reflective community

Examples of good reflective practice do exist, and there are two that readily spring to mind. The first is W. H. Vanstone's classic *Love's Endeavour, Love's Expense*,[8] which he describes as an essay attempting to state what it means to live the 'life of the Church'. What for me is most impressive about the book is the skill with which the author deals with his own insights. His reflections, documented like a skilful theological journal, are sharp insights into the experience of the parish priest in the new parish to which he has been assigned, as they are happening. They are then given space to breathe as he brings other theological insights to bear upon them. If nothing else, it is a wonderful piece of pastoral theologizing.

The other is a more recent book by Rowan Williams, now Archbishop of Canterbury, called *Writing in the Dust*.[9] On its back cover this work is described as a meditation. It is rather more than that, for it is born out of the harrowing experience of witnessing first-hand the events in New York City that we have come to describe only by their date, September 11th. The author was not far from the Twin Towers of the World Trade Center, when two hijacked aeroplanes carrying civilians on domestic flights were flown into the towers by their hijackers, causing their eventual collapse and the known deaths of nearly 3,000 people. What Williams does is not simply to think aloud his ideas, but to spend time describing the experience, reflecting on what it was doing to him and the feelings it evoked in him. It is a struggle with words, both in the descriptive sense and in the desire to apply meaningful thought to tragic events. In doing so the author becomes both vulnerable to criticism, for he treads on the memory of human life, and someone that the reader identifies with, for he says what we have felt but have been unable to pull out of ourselves and share.

> Acknowledging the experience you share is the only thing that opens up the possibility of finding a meaning that can be shared, a language to speak together.[10]

It is a work that is at once profoundly spiritual, human and Christian.

The strengths of these two pieces are apparent. But as examples of reflection they have their weaknesses too. Both are very individualistic in the sense that each author reflects alone. That is certainly what gives the latter a meditative quality. Neither offers any framework for the reflection, and why should they? But what makes them classic works for me is that they make connections. I find that somewhere deep within me I implicitly recognize the truth of what they are saying. There is a different kind of sharing going on. It is this kind of sharing that might open up the possibility of finding a new meaning, as Williams describes, that I hope will be the outcome of this book.

Listening with the ears of God

If this sharing is to happen then there will need to be a concerted effort to listen in a new way. What is documented here is a sample of the experiences of gay and lesbian clergy who live with their partners. If our first reaction to that is one of affront or outrage, because such relationships exist at all, even though many of them existed long before the Lambeth 1998 declaration or the recommendations of *Issues in Human Sexuality* of 1991, then there is not going to be much progress. There may well be some who will desire that. However, if there is to be some kind of response to the challenge to listen to the experience of gay and lesbian people, then the quality of that listening will be crucial. This is a matter not simply of human courtesy, but of theological integrity, for it defines how and who we think we are when we call ourselves the Church. It was an insight Dietrich Bonhoeffer offered to the Church in his work on Christian community and which I would like to quote in full.

> The first service that one owes to others in the fellowship consists in listening to them. Just as love to God begins with listening to his Word, so the beginning of love for the brethren is learning to listen to them. It is God's love for us that he not only gives us his Word, but also lends us his ear. So it is his work that we do for our brother when we learn to listen to him. Christians, especially ministers, so often think that they must always contribute something, when they are in the company of others, that this is the one service that they have to render. They forget that listening can be a greater service than speaking.
>
> Many people are looking for an ear that will listen. They will not find it among Christians, because these Christians are talking where they should be listening. But he who can no longer listen to

his brother will soon be listening no longer to God either; he will be doing nothing but prattle in the presence of God too. This is the beginning of the death of the spiritual life, and in the end there is nothing left but spiritual chatter and clerical condescension arrayed in pious words. One who cannot listen long and patiently will presently be talking beside the point and be never really speaking to others, albeit he be not conscious of it. Anyone who thinks that his time is too valuable to be spent keeping quiet will eventually have no time for God and his brother, but only for himself and his own follies.

Brotherly pastoral care is essentially distinguished from preaching by the fact that, added to the task of speaking the Word, there is the obligation of listening. There is a kind of listening with half an ear that presumes already to know what the other person has to say. It is an impatient, inattentive listening, that despises the brother and is only waiting for a chance to speak and so get rid of the other person. This is no fulfilment of our obligation, and it is certain too that here our attitude toward our brother only reflects our relationship to God. It is little wonder that we are no longer capable of the greatest service of listening that God has committed to us, that of hearing our brother's confession, if we refuse to give ear to our brother on lesser subjects. Secular education today is aware that often a person can be helped merely by having someone who will listen to him seriously, and upon this insight it has constructed its own soul therapy, which has attracted great numbers of people, including Christians. But Christians have forgotten that the ministry of listening has been committed to them by him who is himself the great listener and whose work they should share. We should listen with the ears of God that we may speak the Word of God.[11]

It is amazing to think that Bonhoeffer penned these lines in 1939, before the outbreak of World War Two, for they might easily be the insights of any modern-day pastoral counselling manual. What he describes is a critical insight into any process for reflective practice. So much of the current debate seems to have adopted the characteristic of 'prattling in the presence of God', as Bonhoeffer brilliantly describes it, and so many of the contributors to that cacophony of noise seem to have been the clerical elite who have armed themselves with the rhetoric of 'reflection' without showing the way to participating in it. However, there have been notable exceptions and they deserve some flagging up.

The first is that group of primates and bishops already mentioned, meeting in the aftermath of Lambeth 1998. Whatever else they did, they discovered a respect for their differences by seemingly listening to each other in the way that Bonhoeffer describes. No amount of e-mail can replace the valuable experience of meeting face to face when we are charged with the task of listening, as they themselves recorded. The presumption to know what the other is going to say before they have finished speaking is indeed the overture to spiritual chatter, clerical condescension and the death knell for any kind of spiritual life and true communion with each other. When theological and pastoral reflection is experienced under the threat of declarations that we will be out of communion with each other, we need to ponder what kind of communion we have. This seems to have been something that, as a group, the primates and bishops came to see clearly, and it is something that we can all learn from as the dialogue continues.

The second group to have offered signs of a way forward are the members of Oxford Diocese, who participated in a series of study days to reflect on the document *Issues in Human Sexuality*. Unlike the primates and bishops, they were able to give more time to their study and reflection by creating a lengthier process. Also unlike the primates and bishops (because they are all primates and bishops), they were able to establish a far more diverse group to steer the study days. Theirs included heterosexuals and homosexuals, men and women, academics, clergy and lay people from a variety of church backgrounds and traditions. They took soundings from other dioceses to establish good practice and process and moved forward in a manner that they considered appropriate for their diocesan members without claiming it to be the best way for all. What they discovered, and what I think they offer to anyone else establishing a process for this kind of corporate reflection, was the need to be clear about what goals they wanted to achieve.

> The aim of the process was to listen, actively, to the thoughts, opinions and feelings of others. There was no aim to change people's minds and I do not think that the process did that. It did enable clergy to listen to test their thoughts to others and to understand that, from whatever end of the spectrum one comes, others hold views with great sincerity. The complexity of this whole issue was highlighted. Hearing the voices of those who had had a personal struggle with their faith because of their sexuality, was a humbling, moving experience for many.[12]

The study days were clear as to what the task was. If study was about listening then this was an exercise in gathering information (provided by key note speakers) and gathering insight into how gay and lesbian people feel (provided by the presence of gay and lesbian people as participants in each day), and gathering a broad view of a complex topic (provided by the widest range of traditions and backgrounds they could attract). What was clear was that it was not intended to be a debate in which a prevailing view might become diocesan policy. The atmosphere of fear and irrational hatred that might have been generated through the need to win an argument was thus eliminated because it was quite simply, for them, not the right time or place to make such a resolution.

> In discussion very opposing views were expressed. At no time was there any public conflict, name-calling or animosity, which we had witnessed at some deanery synod meetings.[13]

The third group are the members of the 80 or so parishes that make up the Diocese of New Westminster in the Canadian Anglican Church and their bishop, Michael Ingham.

Whatever position we might hold on the blessing of same-sex unions or reaction we might have to one individual diocese endorsing a rite of blessing for public use, I think that there was something quite commendable about the process that was followed to allow the opportunity for open dialogue and study at every level of diocesan life. There is surely something to learn from this if study and listening is to benefit the whole Church.

The decision to finally go ahead with an authorized diocesan liturgy was passed by the New Westminster diocesan synod in 2002. It took place at the end of the two-day annual meeting at Capilano College in North Vancouver, following a vote in which 62.5 per cent of the lay and clergy delegates upheld the motion, 215 votes to 129. It was not the first time that the synod had examined the issue, having previously voted on it in 1998 and 2001. On both occasions the voting in favour had been less than 60 per cent, and Bishop Ingham had declined to assent to the synod's request on each occasion. In 2002, the synod had made the proposal again but with the following provisions:

- A conscience clause so that no person be compelled to perform or participate in blessing same-sex unions if they believed it was wrong.
- A process in which a parish would have to request by majority vote that it be a place where blessings are performed – otherwise blessings would not be allowed.
- And provision for an 'episcopal visitor' – a conservative bishop to provide pastoral care for priests and parishes who wanted it. Bishop Ingham, however, reserved all his authority as diocesan bishop.

Speaking at the end of the voting, Ingham endorsed these pastoral measures in his summing up.

> We have voted not to compel but to permit, to permit those parishes that wish to celebrate permanent, intimate, loving relationships between persons of the same sex to do so in recognition of the God-given goodness of their sacred mutual commitments.

The authorized rite was devised and first used on 28 May 2003 at St Margaret's Cedar Cottage in East Vancouver, with the Revd Margaret

Marquardt officiating. The couple, Michael Kalmuk and Kelly Mont-fort, both local care workers, had been together for 21 years. Within 48 hours the Archbishop of Nigeria had severed communion with the Diocese of New Westminster and the Archbishop of Canterbury had issued a stern rebuke.

Yet the preparation for this had been going on for years. Following the diocesan synod vote in 1998, just before the Lambeth Conference, Bishop Ingham had withheld his consent and instead issued a six-point plan.

First, he asked the diocesan synod to re-visit the proposal in 2001 following an 18-month period of reflection and dialogue.

Second, he established a system of 'parish twinning' in which each parish was linked with another in a process of learning, listening and study. The parishes were to meet and dialogue every month (except the summer holiday months) and it was to be an exercise that was open to all members of each church. The diocese was to provide training and support to parish leaders and study resources for the dialogue.

Third, in response to the Lambeth Conference, Ingham established what he called a Bishop's Commission on Gay and Lesbian Voices. The commission was to consist of representatives of the gay and lesbian community, along with others. Its mandate was to assist the parishes in hearing the voice and experience of gay and lesbian Christians. He stressed that it was to play a vital role in the dialogue process and every twinned parish was to invite them and hear from them.

Fourth, he would establish a Commission on Faith and Doctrine whose mandate would be to help parishes listen to the voice of Scripture and Church teaching, with both the ears of tradition and the insights of modern biblical and theological scholarship. The commission would provide short study papers discussing the doctrinal and ethical issues raised by same-sex partnerships, referring to specific questions for response. The commission's work would provide the basic written material for study and dialogue.

Fifth, he would establish a Commission on Legal and Canonical Matters with a brief to offer guidance on the question of whether the authority existed for a diocese and bishop to authorize the blessing of same-sex partnerships, upon the resolution of its synod. The commission's findings would be made available for anyone to study within and outside the diocese. The membership of this commission would be drawn from across the entire Canadian Anglican Church, to ensure that the best national as well as local expertise was utilized and to ensure transparency. Ingham stressed that he was keen for the diocese to be seen as not acting independently.

Sixth, the bishop would ask the Bishop's Commission on Liturgy to prepare a rite of blessing for same-sex unions, to be authorized for use in the diocese should the decision to proceed be taken by synod. This, he stressed, was not to pre-empt any outcome of the process and debate, but rather more to satisfy the desire to know in advance what such a rite of blessing would look like if they were to proceed. This commission was to consult with the Faith and Doctrine Commission to develop the appropriate theology for the rite. They were also to draw up guidelines for the admission and pastoral preparation for such couples seeking the Church's blessing on their relationship and for long-term support afterwards.

In conclusion, the bishop encouraged patience, study and dialogue, and active participation in the process.

> I am asking the diocese to continue the study, to continue the dialogue. I am proposing that we move forward slowly, that we move forward together, but that we keep moving. The process will take a full two years. It will require the active participation of every Anglican, of every point of view.

The aims of the Diocese of New Westminster were rather different from those of the Diocese of Oxford in the long term. Theirs was to equip a diocesan synod with whatever was necessary to make an informed decision as a synod that would affect church life at grass roots level, without making claims for any other part of the Canadian Anglican Church. It is clear that these aims were not appreciated by some of the Canadian bishops. The Bishop of Nova Scotia considered 62.5 per cent an insufficient majority, the Archbishop of Saskatoon described it as a matter not for a diocesan synod but for the General

Synod of Canada, and the Bishop of Fredericton expressed concern for Church unity. Others saw the outcome differently. The Bishop of Niagara described the decision as courageous, the Bishop of Keewatin declared his respect for the decision though not wanting it for his own diocese, and the Primate of the Anglican Church in Canada declared that New Westminster and their bishop had acted responsibly in introducing the blessings to the diocese.

No one made any criticism of the process that the diocese had followed to pray and study together. Whatever personal view we might hold on the entire subject of conferring God's blessing through authorized rituals of the Church, I think that the objective to establish openness and transparency in realizing those aims is highly commendable.

The real problem for the Diocese of New Westminster was that they dared to address the issue at all as a diocese. They were not the first to look at the whole matter of services of blessing for gay and lesbian couples; a small number of dioceses in the United States of America had already done so. What seems to have been highlighted in the case of New Westminster is what happens when your commitment to openness and transparency is implemented on a wider Church stage. It seems to be a lamentable and all too common feature of the Church, which ought to be committed to openness, that instead it finds it hard to live with. The Church of England is particularly susceptible to this. It is an institution that makes its upper level appointments through secretive systems rather than the openness of an electoral or other process. It has managed to get by since the publication of *Issues in Human Sexuality* through the adoption of an unwritten agreement between bishops and gay clergy that the one won't ask if the other doesn't tell. What kind of platform is this for a relationship that is meant to be pastoral? How can we hope for honesty in the face of such institutional secrecy?

The kind of study and reflective process that New Westminster has undertaken is something that inevitably draws hostility because it shines a light on the hiddenness and secrecy of a way of life that one group of people have had to endure for generations. Furthermore it points the finger at the dishonesty of the well-dressed compromise

that 'don't ask me and I won't tell you' really is. Where New Westminster's experience is particularly powerful is that it is made not
through a singular reflection of one theologian, mystic or crank who
can easily be dismissed, but through the consensual cooperation of
the body of Christ in one place. It is a corporate act. It is a discernment
that has been made by a body of believers. The response of fear to
exposure is one of threat. So, participation in any kind of reflective
exercise that might supply new insights to the participants is bound
to invite criticism from some quarters and outright rejection from
others.

Perfect love drives out fear

So each of these groups offers different insights into the benefits of
reflective practice. The primates group tells us that listening face to
face is the first step to casting out fear. If there is to be any chance of
making progress beyond the awkward question, it needs to be in the
personal encounter, where the human experience of gay relationships can be heard without being pronounced upon, and the fears
that others have that issues of doctrine, sacrament and scripture
might be compromised will also be heard. The Oxford diocesan study
group shows us that there needs to be a willingness to gather information and new insights from others with whom we do not share the
same position. There must be some incentive to face this issue, rather
than ignore it in the hope that it will go away, or sideline it by declaring that there are other, more pressing issues that we should be concerning ourselves with. The Diocese of New Westminster tells us that
a transparent, detailed process, which keeps everyone in the picture
as to where they have got to and what the next steps are to be, is
important. There must also be commitment to engaging as many as
possible to the reflective journey and a good deal of patience as it is
made. These examples also remind us that even with provision for
those who follow the process but cannot live with the findings, there
will be some casualties. The larger the body involved in the reflection,
the more likely this will be.

All three groups show us that reflective practice is not only possible and worthwhile, but also essential if we are to grow together into the mind of Christ. They also show us that it is time-consuming and an extremely difficult thing to do.

This chapter has been necessarily theoretical for the larger part. In Chapter 3 we start to hear the experiences of gay and lesbian lives that have not only decided to stay in the Church but have felt called to serve it through ordination to the diaconate and priesthood. As we listen through the words on the page, we will need to keep reminding ourselves that although this is not the face-to-face dialogue of the suggested reflective process, neither are we simply reading research data material. The narratives supplied belong to real lives. So we will need to try to get inside those lives as if they were in the same room as us. Here they are.

Notes

1 T. S. Eliot, *The Four Quartets*, Faber and Faber, 2001.
2 Jeffrey Heskins, *Unheard Voices*, Darton, Longman and Todd, 2001.
3 T. Latter, *Charlton Parish Magazine*, July 1996.
4 *Unheard Voices*, p. 117.
5 *Issues in Human Sexuality*, 5:16, p. 45.
6 Elaine Graham, Editorial, *Crucible*, Sept–Dec 2003.
7 J. Woodward and S. Pattison (eds), *The Blackwell Reader in Pastoral and Practical Theology*, Blackwell, 2000, p. 135.
8 W. H. Vanstone, *Love's Endeavour, Love's Expense*, Darton, Longman and Todd, 1977.
9 Rowan Williams, *Writing in the Dust*, Hodder and Stoughton, 2002.
10 *Writing in the Dust*, p. 73.
11 Dietrich Bonhoeffer, *Life Together*, SCM Press, 1972, pp. 75–6.
12 Jo Saunders, *Some Issues in Human Sexuality*, Church House Publishing, 2003, Appendix, p. 325.
13 *Some Issues in Human Sexuality*, p. 325.

3

To have and to hold from this day

THE SEARCH FOR MEANINGFUL COMMITMENT

There are times when we come across another person with whom there is an immediate connection. Whatever that connection, be it an easy manner, a physical attraction, a sense of humour or an intellectual engagement, there is usually a sense of enjoyment and excitement in making such a discovery. Most of us take meeting others for granted. There are usually ample opportunities in a lifetime for such connections to occur and although for some they never develop into anything else, for many there are the occasions when such moments of connection are looked back on as defining moments. They are experiences that begin a change of course in our lives. Sometimes that defining moment is the genesis of what is to become a relationship or partnership that is so particular, it becomes exclusive to that other person. It shares itself intimately and privately, but manifests itself publicly. At least that is the assumed way in which such relationships find acceptance in our social and public circles for 89 per cent of the UK population. The possibilities for openness and transparency have culminated in a culture that is now widely accepting of many couples living together and of others adopting the long-established traditions of marriage.

For the other 11 per cent, public commitment is not so straightforward, although in some Western European and North American cultures life together for the gay or lesbian couple has become very much better than even a generation ago. There are exceptions. Religious institutions including numerous churches have adopted rigorous policies condemning all kinds of gay and lesbian lifestyles other than the single and chaste variety. Some even offer programmes of deliverance and healing for those of a homosexual orientation.

For the gay couple wanting to live an open life within the Church of England there is some hope of official acceptance and even recognition. Many churches report couples worshipping in their congregations who form essential and much valued parts of those communities. Faithful and open same-sex partnerships are commended for support within the local church in the Bishops' statement, *Issues in Human Sexuality*:

> . . . we do not reject those who sincerely believe it [a faithful monogamous relationship with another of the same sex] is God's call to them. We stand alongside them in the fellowship of the Church, all alike dependent on the undeserved grace of God. All those who seek to live their lives in Christ owe one another friendship and understanding. It is therefore important that in every congregation such homophiles should find fellow Christians who will sensitively and naturally provide this for them. Indeed, if it is not done, any professions on the part of the Church that it is committed to openness and learning about the homophile situation can be no more than empty words.[1]

It is a section of the statement which drifts towards, but stops short of affirming, the union of partners of the same sex as a 'calling'. Instead, it offers the benefit of the doubt that such couples live together in the hope of growing in love for God and thus, if not quite commended, is certainly not to be rejected out of ignorance.

> . . . there are others who are conscientiously convinced that this way of abstinence is not the best for them, and that they have more hope of growing in love for God and neighbour with the help of a loving and faithful homophile partnership, in intention lifelong, where mutual self-giving includes the physical expression of their attachment.[2]

So openness and honesty are at the very least tolerated for same-sex Christian couples who are regular members of our congregations. However, such is not the case for the clergy, who are consigned to lives of solitary celibacy or platonic friendships, whether they feel called to such an estate or not. The bishops argue for the exclusion of the clergy from such partnerships on the grounds that it will diminish their pastoral function. In other words, they infer that should such relationships make life difficult for those the clergy minister to, it is undesirable and therefore unacceptable.[3]

What this declaration does is merely compound the climate of suspicion, create the dishonest pastoral relationship of 'don't ask, don't tell', and leave no freedom to discover the legitimacy of such claims. How are we ever going to learn from the experience of such men and women if we insist that they collude with this dishonest cloaking device? Clearly there are a good number of clergy who are living in well-supported partnerships for whom the secrecy has become intolerable. Theirs has been a search for meaningful commitment in a wider church context of double standards. This might be all right for the laity, but not for the clergy, says the report, because some of the rest of the laity might not like it, even though they are being told to create meaningful Christian fellowship with gay and lesbian lay members who might want to be part of their communities. It just doesn't add up.

To have and to hold

To have and to hold are, of course, the well-known words of assent and commitment drawn from the marriage service. They are powerful words because they indicate the desire for security and affectionate intimacy. To have someone in your life implies a relationship of both positive owning and of a sense of belonging to another. To hold and be held by them further suggests a protection of that belonging. They are terms that rightly define the relationship of monogamous commitment. I use them in this instance not to make a case for gay and lesbian marriage, but because they best describe the desire of those clergy and ordinands who shared their insights and reflections on their partnerships. In what seems to be an impossible context for gay and lesbian clergy, the search for commitment has motivated them and the discovery of security and intimate affection has enabled them to break through this context and live within it. For some, meeting their partners has been the transformation of their lives and the renaissance of their ministry. For others, the change has been less dramatic, but still nonetheless significant.

> *I wasn't at all convinced that I wanted to be in a relationship, because I was well on the way through the selection process for ordination. But it became very clear to me that God was presenting me with someone with whom I could learn an enormous amount. Most importantly from whom I could learn to love. I have realized without a shadow of a doubt that not only am I not called to celibacy, I am not called to be a single priest. What I will gain from the stability of a loving, challenging, warm relationship where I have to more and more open my heart to somebody will add enormously to my ministry as a priest.*
>
> *Female ordinand with partner 18 months*

> *We met 15 years ago through a mutual friend within a church context and at that stage both of us were fairly good evangelicals trying to think about what it meant to be Christian and to be gay, and therefore to try and live a celibate life. We didn't live together at first but after a few years we reached the stage where it was a strain to organize our lives at a distance, and since deciding to live together our relationship has deepened. Both of us are people who don't thrive on our own, and loneliness was a feature of earlier times.*
>
> *Male priest with partner 15 years*

The sense of finding another in an otherwise repressive institutional context, with the fear of offending ecclesial authorities or others in the church neighbourhood, often brings a feeling of relief. There is no doubt that for many, the self-discovery of their gay or lesbian orientation and the desire to continue to live and work out a Christian vocation within the Church can create a sense of anxiety and loneliness. What will people think? Is it all too much trouble to try and explain? Is it better to remain quiet and solitary and avoid the awkward questions? Will my career in the Church be advanced or diminished if I am open about myself? If I met someone, what would I do about it anyway?

From my point of view, she came to the parish at a time when I had more or less come to the conclusion that although I wasn't in a relationship with anybody, it felt as if I was hiding. It was coming towards the time when I wanted to tell friends that I was gay. Nobody knew. I hadn't told anybody. So she was a fresh face and therefore it was a good opportunity to talk about it and what the implications were and everything else. She was the first person I told in the church or anywhere.

Partner to female priest 2 years

Couples like this met in a variety of ways. Some met through newspaper columns, one couple met through the internet, one couple met on a retreat, two others met on holiday, one met at a women's refuge, one met through work together in the parish, several met at theological college or on a training course and a significant number were introduced by mutual friends at a social occasion. Most couples live together all or most of the time. Several maintain two homes and share their time between them and one couple, because of their work commitments, have to live in different countries and make particular efforts to create regular time through the year to see each other.

Unsurprisingly, most lived in urban areas, though some lived in suburbia, one couple lived in a provincial town and two couples lived in rural villages. However, while there was a sense that it was much easier to be gay in the city, to be part of a huge and impersonal urban sprawl in which anyone could hide, there was no sense among any of the couples of wanting to be hidden. Indeed, the contrast between the openness that many described in their parishes and the wider parish community, and that of the Church institution and those governing it, was quite stark. For some it is a considerable struggle to live with the two tensions.

We are in the middle of a metropolitan city. I have been 'out' in every aspect of my life for many, many years so becoming involved with a priest has meant, in some respect, putting a foot back in the closet, which I struggle with on an ongoing basis.

Partner to male priest 7 years

For others, the context in which they found themselves was one of local acceptance.

> *This is very much an old-fashioned, back-street, blue-collar parish. Ninety-eight per cent are white British and the church is Anglo-Catholic. It is fairly right wing, has a Conservative MP and some Old Labour elements to it. Having said all that, it only serves as a background. For example, there is another gay couple who live across the road. They live quite openly and are very accepted in the back street they live in.*
>
> *Male priest with partner 2 years*

> *We live in a suburban area which is predominantly middle class. This context affects to some degree the way in which we are able to live together. There is a large proportion of families with children and before we moved here we were a bit worried that a lot of the myths about gay people and paedophilia would have some negative impact. But in fairness, that hasn't really happened.*
>
> *Male priest with partner 15 years*

> *It is a typical country house for the region it is in. We are known as a couple by our neighbours and the people we meet.*
>
> *Male ordinand with partner 5 years*

> *The overall parish environment is a fairly liberal one. Most people have gay friends at work or at the university or wherever. It's not a great threat to them. Having said that, the elderly resident population also seem to have had contact with gay people in the past. Certainly at this church there was a couple who were very active in the church, now both dead, who were certainly recognized as a partnership – not that anyone would have called it that.*
>
> *Male priest with partner 8 years*

Still others found that this sense of acceptance in the local community went beyond the notion of toleration, to one of active welcome and hospitality. They were seen not only as integral members of the local community, but as valued and essential features of the same. The context that was their local parish neighbourhood was non-judgemental,

39

open and caring, and looking out for each other as neighbours. Many expressed surprise at the degree of openness and warmth they experienced from neighbours and other local community residents, who recognized their partnership, acknowledged it and welcomed them, making them feel valued.

> Our next door but one neighbour was introducing us to the other neighbours, 'This is the new vicar and his partner and this is their son.' I'd never met this woman before and she said, 'That's nice. Are you going to have lodgers?' The previous incumbent had had the house stuffed with lodgers. 'No,' I said. 'Just the family.' She replied, 'Oh, that's nice, a normal family.' A normal family! I was speechless that people's expectations were so different.
>
> Male priest with partner 5 years

> I live in a terraced house in a multicultural, inner-city context. I don't feel judged or watched. My neighbours are aware of my relationship but completely accepting of it.
>
> Female ordinand with partner 18 months

> We live in a terraced house in a mixed area. My partner was previously married and had two children from that marriage. One has left home and the other is still living with us. Next door is a gay man who lives separately from his partner. The community is quite close and we all look out for each other. It is a good community feeling.
>
> Female priest with partner 13 years

> The context is certainly not one in which he has to come in under the cover of darkness and park the car several streets away.
>
> Male priest with partner 20 years

So much of the social setting and the context of what it means to live in an accepting and sustaining neighbourhood goes into the foundations of the building of a stable relationship. The sense of gratitude for this context is apparent and seems to be the chief provider of the confidence to live openly within the church community. There is an

assumption among many that the gay lifestyle is an entirely promiscuous one, and this is extended to the entire gay and lesbian population by those who continue to promote this view. From the sample of
clergy, ordinands and partners interviewed, it was clear that many
were aware of the view, but most found that this lifestyle lay a long
way from the stability that they were seeking for their own well-being
and the good of the church communities that they had been called to
serve. What is clear is that promiscuity is unhealthy, abusive and
destructive. Sexual intimacy with several partners is often accompan-
ied by lying and deceit and cannot lay the foundations for stability
and mature growth.

Closely related to this assumption is the view that those who wish
to be open about their partnerships do so merely to 'rock the boat',
like unruly children who cannot bear to get their own way. Indeed,
the tone adopted in *Issues in Human Sexuality* in addressing such relationships is not dissimilar to such a view. Clergy who are open about
their homosexual orientation but who live single lives, abstaining
from sexual intercourse, are applauded. Those church communities
who cannot accept such honourable candour in their clergy are not
worthy of the name of Christian, we are told.[4] Those who are in active
partnerships and choose to be open about them are respected for
their integrity, but advised to abide by the directives of the manual,
namely to desist from such relationships. To continue to live openly
is seen as pre-emptive action within the movement for change in the
Church's perceptions and teachings.

This is an interesting take on the dynamics of honest relationships.
It allows no room for exploring the possibility of the fallibility of this
position that the writers fully admit to elsewhere.[5] Of those surveyed
for this book, all wished to be open and honest about their relationship with their partner and the search for stability. But by the same
token all were mindful of and sensitive to a realization not only that
the Church was not of one mind on the matter, but also that the largest
part of the Church had not had the opportunity to express its opinion
on the subject. Instead, they gave their quiet insights into how they
thought they were perceived as gay and lesbian clergy within their
own communities. None would describe themselves as living with a

partner simply out of protest to the Church and its official position on same-sex partnerships. All who were undertaking the search for stability were doing so because they saw it as life-enhancing. That their openness was challenging to this position is secondary. However, it is indeed a challenge, and one that might be better met with a listening ear and a review of what we currently know about such relationships and their impact on Christian and wider parish communities, than with the cry of 'Foul'.

What same-sex clergy partners were able to tell us in this particular overview is that they have great respect for the communities they serve, and tread gently when dealing with their openness.

> *In the parish I am as open as I can be. If people ask, I always answer. I think that when people ask a direct question they deserve an answer. I think that people get to know, not by osmosis, but by us being around. We have dinners and people come and they get introduced. Word goes round, but I don't go around flag-waving.*
>
> Male priest with partner 8 years

By the same token there was a good deal of evidence that couples were often well accepted within the local communities that they served and lived in. This was an important insight, as one of the chief concerns of the Bishops' report was that clergy could not be accorded the same privilege of living openly with a partner of the same sex as it would be a cause of scandal to the faith community they were to lead.

> *In the parish from week one my partner was welcomed without any introduction from me. So any hope of keeping it quiet was not really very realistic. So we don't conceal, but neither do we thrust who we are in people's faces.*
>
> Male priest with partner 15 years

> *We are entirely open. We made our home in this parish as a couple from the very first. Nobody ever batted an eyelid and we were made extremely welcome. They were the same people who encouraged me to go forward for ordination.*
>
> Male priest with partner 32 years

Our friends all know and they are members of the parish community. Those others who know are openly supportive. Where it is more difficult is with those people you have assumed have worked it out, but nothing has been said. There was a good example of this last Christmas when a woman in the congregation gave me a Christmas present and said it was for both of us. Nothing was said before or since, but it seemed pretty clear from this that we were assumed to be a couple. She had been someone I was most anxious about offending or upsetting. So that was lovely.

Female priest with partner 2 years

One priest admitted that there was one member of his congregation who had, to his knowledge, left the church community and gone to another on account of his open relationship. But by and large everyone else gave accounts of support and even approval. If there was anything scandalous to be found it might be the stark contrast between the acceptance and acceptability found at grass roots level and the fear of rejection at other levels of the Church. Some described the sense of incredulity of their wider parish community upon learning what an issue this was for the Church. For many of those unfamiliar with the debate, the lack of openness in the Church seemed strange in comparison with the high degree of openness they found in the community. Ironically, one incumbent described this openness as a potential banana-skin for him. The very openness he applauded from without the Church might lead to difficulties within the Church because of its guardedness.

The stuff I most fear in this context is born of the fact that on the whole people round here are very accepting (of who I am) and so don't realize that this is an issue for the Church. I remember speaking to someone at one of the local schools who could not believe that there was any kind of problem. Because she didn't realize what an issue it was, she was able to talk about things very naturally and normally. Ironically that [her openness] could cause all kinds of problems with the people who find the issue difficult.

Male priest with partner 15 years

Ordinands training for ministry or about to go to selection conferences gave a mixed reaction. Most found enormous support from
within their sponsoring parish communities. Often these had been
congregations which they had grown up in or had come to as a
couple and which had never known them as anything other than a
couple. Some described open support from their Diocesan Director
of Ordinands, and others whose responsibility it was to steer them
through the process of selection and training. In some cases this
support extended through the training period.

> *I haven't kept any of this relationship secret apart from on the guidance of my
> Director of Ordinands. I was lucky enough to be put on a placement in a
> parish where the vicar immediately read my situation. We had an early dis-
> cussion about my relationship and I was able to tell her that I was in the
> Church not despite my sexuality but because of my experiences as a gay person.
> The whole parish community have been entirely supportive and aware of the
> dynamics. However, I have been counselled not to make a sacrifice of myself.
> The most I fear is that after all this openness and honesty at grass roots, the
> diocesan bishop will refuse to ordain me.*
>
> Female ordinand with partner 1 year

> *I have had no reason not to be open in the past and that remained so until I
> entered the ordination process. Most of my parish placements have been in
> rural districts or provincial towns and so I try not to be in their face about it,
> but when my partner visits, he comes with me to worship and I introduce him
> afterwards and leave it open as to who he is.*
>
> Male ordinand with partner 5 years

It is that moment of entering the ordination process that is the
defining one. There is a switch from an accepting reality to one that is
covert and guarded to a debilitating degree. One ordinand described
a general conversation with some married women ordinands who
were talking about their wedding and engagement rings and how the
moment of decision to marry had affected their lives. They had been
comparing their jewellery and sharing stories of how their husbands

had reacted to their call to ordination. She was unable to participate in this conversation for fear of exposure and recrimination. She could neither show them her ring, the sign of her partner's pledge of fidelity, nor could she speak openly of the woman who had given it to her more than ten years previously.

Another ordinand described how he had trained on a regional ordination scheme in which support was offered throughout to spouses and partners. He had thought this quite progressive thinking, and had looked forward to sharing some of the attention that training and ultimately ordination would bring with his partner. At the first weekend, however, it became apparent that the offer was really only for heterosexual married and boyfriend/girlfriend couples. One of the college staff advised his partner that such occasions were not for him. For those who were so used to open acceptance in their sponsoring parishes, this was a burdensome adjustment to make.

> I had been in my home parish for 25 years and they all know my partner. I have similarly always been open about my sexuality in the workplace, but when I went forward for ordination training, it came as a big shock to me when I couldn't talk about it any more. I couldn't talk about her and I couldn't talk about our family because it was made clear to me that if you drew attention to it then the bishop would be informed. Those were the rules, so the best thing was to keep your mouth shut. I found that very hard.
>
> Female ordinand with partner 13 years

In the field of public ministry, this tension has the potential to wreak destruction on the very relationships that are sustaining them. What is it about an institution that seeks to offer support and encouragement to countless numbers of people who choose to remain outside its membership but does not provide the transparency to sustain its own ministers? Some couples realized at an early stage that in this climate the worst that could actually happen was to be found out. But what they really feared was the combustion of their relationship because of the strain of the secrecy.

I think that both of us would be more fearful of the Church destroying our relationship than of simply being found out. For me that would be my biggest concern, because I don't think that I am doing anything that I shouldn't do and if the Church can't cope with that then there might come a point when I would have to say that enough was enough. So I think that my bigger fear would be that simply living the way that we do would be sufficient pressure to break us up, though that doesn't mean to say that I would want to lose my job.

Female priest with partner 3 years

The power of ritual and blessing

In his classic book on human sexuality, *Embodiment*, James Nelson asks the question why those who are seeking to live lives of faithfulness and stability within our communities should be denied access to the sustaining and supporting rituals of the Church.[6] It is something we look to encourage in advocating the purposes of marriage. In that particular institution we are advised that such rituals strengthen publicly the very elements of what it means to live a married life. In it there is a consecration of sexual union, the possibility of stable family life and the enshrinement of companionship, all of which takes place within the wider context of living openly in the community. Marriage is not a personal thing, as somebody once tried to persuade me. It is a very public thing, which is why the decision to undertake it is often a very nerve-racking one to make.

Those of us who preside at such rituals as devised by the Church know that those who participate in them are often deeply moved by the experience. The bride and groom, who stammer through their words or shake nervously in placing the ring, often say so when the ordeal is over and the registers are signed. Such official Church ceremonial does not exist for gay and lesbian couples, other than in a few dioceses in Canada and North America and opinion was divided among the clergy and ordinands as to the value of public ritual.

Some had undertaken a private ceremony, in what they felt was 'sacred space', where they had exchanged vows, and marked the occasion with an exchange of rings.

We bought each other a ring and went to a chapel run by a religious community and sat by ourselves and exchanged rings. So in that sense we plighted our troth to each other. That was about 17 years ago, but we haven't done a public ceremony yet. We are minded to do that when it becomes a legal entity. We have already lined up which bishops we can invite to the Town Hall and which will do the blessing!

Male priest with partner 20 years

Others had done similarly in more social and informal space.

We didn't to begin with and in fact not until relatively recently did we actually have any kind of thing to mark the beginning of our relationship. We have discussed what it would mean. Yet because we are products of the society we live in we do find the need to mark it in some way.

Male ordinand with partner 6 years

We did have a ceremony of sorts, which was in my flat. We had a few friends round and we made a declaration of commitment to each other. There was no priest to oversee it.

Male priest with partner 5 years

Others hadn't and had thought better of it since embarking on their relationship, while some were in the throes of thinking about it and examining how it might be achieved. One couple hadn't at the outset, but had sought to do so at a significant anniversary. They had been thwarted by internal local church disagreements and ultimately called the ceremony off. One couple were emphatic that they wouldn't until such a ceremony was given some legal teeth!

If the law in this country changed in our favour and asked of us some sort of commitment service (though I wouldn't call it a marriage), I would want to go down that route.

Male partner of priest 20 years

47

So this significant sample of clergy, in full knowledge of the power of public ritual, have, to a man and woman, declined to create the opportunity for themselves to be strengthened in their partnerships in this way. Why?

It might be attributed to the political climate. One couple who had been together since the early 1970s declared that they had not participated in a ceremony because it had not been knowingly available to them, even privately and behind closed doors. Others had simply been getting on with the business of life together for so long now it seemed an odd declaration to be making, other than at the start of a significant relationship.

For most, however, it came down to what they thought they understood marriage to be, or to have become. Recent studies of marriage indicate that before the eighteenth century marriage was a state that couples grew towards. Communities were smaller and when couples became married it was a mark of community recognition. X and Y were recognized as a couple. The Solemnization of Matrimony was just that. It was not merely a marriage service, but a sacred declaration and commitment before God of something *already* recognized by the local community.[7] It remains the case that it doesn't need the clergy to make a marriage, since it is the couple who marry each other and in so doing become ministers to each other.

For the couples here, there was concern that whether or not they felt their relationship was as binding for them as any marriage, or analogous to their understanding of Christian marriage, they were keen not to confuse public perceptions of what they thought their relationship was. Having said that, once stripped of the term 'marriage' and the language of marriage, many felt bereft of a term to describe the most important relationship of their lives.

> *He is my partner and I delight in that and that there is a publicness to it. I also know that in the present climate, once we attach the word marriage publicly it confuses issues. Theologically I think that marriage is a particular construct which I don't think is appropriate theologically between two people of the same sex.*
>
> *Male priest with partner 18 months*

I think my partnership is like a marriage, and I know it is for him. It's just the problem of the word 'marriage' when transposed onto gay relationships.

Male priest with partner 6 years

For a significant proportion of the couples, and particularly the women, marriage as a heterosexual institution is perceived to be in itself in trouble. This is not a reason to circumnavigate it, but rather to look carefully at why. The women are clear that the positives in marriage are there for all to see.

In terms of what I believe marriage is about, serving God in one another, commitment, learning, growing, opening up; all those things are there, but as a concept marriage isn't there for either of us.

Female ordinand with partner 18 months

But historically, as a concept marriage has not accorded women an egalitarian relationship with their husbands. In the Book of Common Prayer they are to obey and serve their husbands, who are not obliged to avow the same in return. For many this has created a stereotype of relationship that is unsustainable and unhelpful in the same sex partnership.

I think that marriage is a heterosexual thing and it makes assumptions of us to use that model. People say things like 'Who is the man in your relationship?' Those kinds of stereotypes are not particularly helpful.

Female partner to priest 13 years

It is not a marriage because gender politics do make a difference in marriages and one of the wonderful things about a gay partnership is that you work things out in a way that in a marriage I think you often just take for granted. So we have to discuss who washes the car and who runs the bank account, how we spend and share our money and how we make decisions generally. There is no assumption that I am the husband and she is the wife.

Female priest with partner 2 years

I am not particularly bothered about using the term 'marriage'. I am as committed to her as if I were married to her. I am in this for life. I actually think that there are problems for marriage as it has been understood traditionally. I even think that maybe gay and lesbian relationships have something to say and some input into that. Certainly the element of mutuality and equality is more taken for granted in those relationships, whereas the Church still struggles to throw off some of the baggage that comes with traditional ideas of marriage.

Female priest with partner 3 years

So the language of the open gay and lesbian partnership tends not to identify itself with the institution of marriage *per se*, which is contrary to the accusation that is often made, namely that such committed partnerships are undermining of marriage. From this sample, that seems not to be the case. If anything, such partnerships are enhancing the idea of the marital partnership by endorsing the need for stability and faithfulness and advocating openness and public acceptance, at the same time seeking to offer insights, from a different perspective, of what it means to live in a committed intimate sexual union. While not enjoying the social stability and openness of the marital union, these partnerships affirm marriage and model themselves, in a different way, on what it means to be openly together. However, as we have seen, this leaves these couples, living within the Church, quite vulnerable. So where do they find support?

Shall we keep it in the family?

Being open and honest about a partnership with another of the same sex seems to be as difficult within the family as it is within the Church and, as within the Church, couples looking to find support for their partnerships reported varying degrees of acceptance. What was particularly interesting was the marked contrast in the levels of acceptance from one generation to another.

Older couples with parents still living indicated that their parents had often had difficulty in accepting that their children were gay. This was particularly the case with fathers. One couple described how the father of the family had for his entire lifetime been unable to accept the partnership. In death, and out of habitual loyalty to her deceased husband, his widow continued to receive both men with courtesy in her household, but made no public acknowledgement of her son in partnership with another man. The framed family photographs in the living room showed his siblings with their spouses or partners and children, but all photographs of him were of him alone.

There were exceptions to this, examples of couples whose parents 'came round' to accepting that their child was gay and in a partnership with another man or woman. In nearly every case it was the mother who mended the fences that needed to be fixed. Those that described a growing acceptance told the story in generous tones. On those occasions where parents had made the transition, accepting that their son or daughter was different from what they had anticipated or even hoped for, the journey to a new acceptance was never ultimately begrudging.

We are very much part of his brother's family. I preached at his niece's wedding and I have conducted a number of family funerals, including his father. His mother treats me just like another son and introduces me to people as his partner. It is very okay. A nice quiet sort of acceptance, but very warm.

Male priest with partner 32 years

Younger clergy found that their parents and families, once aware of what it was like for them, changed their perspective on the Church's official line. Some were protective and concerned how their son or daughter would be affected by what they saw as an aggressive line by the Church leadership. Others felt frustration at seeing the Church struggle miserably with the whole notion of gay and lesbian relationships in abstract and theoretical terms, while it was actually making decisions that affected the lives of their children.

I think that my parents are quite scared for me in my relationship because they have seen the hostility of the Church to gays in the papers recently. So I think that they are concerned that this step will bring me a lot of emotional pain, but they are entirely supportive.

Female ordinand with partner 1 year

My parents live in a very rural part of Cornwall and when I told my mother a number of years ago, she made me promise not to tell my father. In the heat of the moment I agreed to do that. However, I feel pretty sure that he knows. During the Jeffrey John saga she was talking to me on the phone and saying things like, 'Well, I hope that the Church is going to grow up.' So there is something of a shift going on.

Male priest with partner 15 years

One family divided down the generational line in its response to one of its members living in an open lesbian relationship.

My family have lived in the same small town all their lives and I don't think they have really grasped the concept at all. I think that they are pretty much the same as some of the parish. They think that I have moved into the vicarage because it is a big place. That's the older ones. The younger ones are fine. They have understood and are okay about it.

Female partner to priest 2 years

So the families of the couples reveal a slow sea change in attitudes and ways of relating to those members of their own family who are gay and who introduce their partners. Most offer a generous welcome; some find themselves on a journey in which they rethink principles and values. They often move to a new place in their assessment of gay and lesbian partnerships, because they have to absorb the experience at first hand. Talk of orientation and genital acts becomes a non-sensical way of thinking about gay and lesbian relationships when it is your own brother or child. Some, of a much older generation when gay relationships were not given a social airing, remain unable to deal with the matter and live in silent denial. The worst is outright rejection, and although there were some examples of this, they were few and far between. Families, for openly gay and lesbian clergy, tend to be places of security that keep a watchful eye on the Church.

Shall we look for it in the local church?

The story was not dissimilar in the local church. Participants in the interview process painted a picture of a church membership that was surprisingly well informed and in step with the social context in which they were immersed. Clergy working in urban areas found this particularly so, and those working in the field of chaplaincy, where the overwhelming majority of those they engaged with did not espouse any formally practised faith, found the greatest degree of acceptance and support. A school chaplain found that his ministry was enhanced, because the students respected his openness and recognized that this was a difficult position to hold in the current climate of the Church.

> *A number of people at school are very pleased about it, because it makes me more human, if you like. I can't be part of the judgemental superior image of what Christian priests are about. That I am a gay man with a partner means that I must be okay. As far as the other members of the Religious Studies department are concerned, not all of them know, but those that do don't seem to have a problem with it. My line manager on the senior management team, who is my mentor, is actually a conservative evangelical, so for him it is actually a bit of a problem, but he recognizes that within the school and their commitment to equal opportunities, it does make me fit into the ethos of the institution.*

> *Male priest with partner 5 years*

A number of others engaged in chaplaincy within a secular context were able to say something similar.

In parish community life, the experience of having a gay or lesbian priest, or a gay or lesbian ordinand working and gaining experience in the parish, seemed to be of secondary importance to members of congregations who were in that situation.

> *I had a conversation with someone recently who told me how much he supported me in my process to ordination. As far as being openly gay in the Church was concerned, he thought I had done a really good job of being myself*

in the parish, and that if I continued to be open and friendly in the way that I had, then the issue of my sexuality would be very secondary, as it had been for him. That is fairly typical of what I have come across.

Female ordinand with partner 18 months

This experience repeated itself right across the board. City clergy found overwhelming support and a singular lack of concern about their sexual orientation, or whether or not they shared their life with a partner. Most told of how members of the congregation would invite them and their partners to social events in their homes, and some clergy went to deanery events with their partners. The overriding concern was considered to be whether they were faithful in serving the communities that had called them.

It is a very mixed congregation and nobody cares. All that they care about is that they are loved and that they are looked after.

Male priest with partner 5 years

You only have to have eyes and ears to know that I am gay, and therefore in one sense there are a good number that know. I would say that they are all very concerned about our well-being. They are more concerned pastorally for us than anything to do with theology. So if I am good to them and to the community then they will be good to me.

Male priest with partner 1 year

Clergy working in suburban districts discovered that the novelty value of a gay vicar and partner soon wore off and most people just got on with life as usual.

They have come to see that there is nothing to regard. There is nothing untoward in the two of us. If they do, they haven't let us know and it really isn't that kind of parish.

Male priest with partner 20 years

In rural districts the story was not so very different.

The village is very well organized and when we first came here we went to a welcoming party for newcomers. There were about 90 people from the village. They seemed to know exactly who we were and were genuinely interested in us. They wanted to know what we were doing and there were a variety of views about it (lifestyle), none of which were hostile. Some were along the lines of well, we don't really go along with this, but I have experienced people being warm and friendly and it not being an issue for them.

Male priest with partner 6 years

What will we say to the bishop?

As gay and lesbian partnerships become a fuller part of social consciousness, it is perhaps not much of a surprise to find that although families sometimes struggle to come to terms with some members being attracted to and living with partners of the same sex, most find a way of holding the difficulties and addressing them. It is also not very surprising that evidence shows that those local church communities who have a gay or lesbian priest, with or without a partner, will to a greater or lesser extent find a way of meeting the issue. Although some of those surveyed had experienced rejection and disapproval at some level, this was not in the church congregations they had since found their way to. It is clear that for some congregations the idea of an openly gay or lesbian partnership within either the membership or the leadership is not acceptable.

One person shared an experience of this. She had been a charismatic and nurtured in the evangelical part of the Anglican Church. Here she had encountered a different kind of reaction when she began to speak openly about herself.

I previously went to a very lively evangelical church and it was a style of worship that I felt very comfortable in. It was popular and had loads of people going to it. However, when I gradually and quietly came out to people, I didn't get smiled at and support. I got nonplussed reactions and people wanted to challenge me. Eventually I knew it was no longer the place for me.

Female ordinand with partner 18 months

Those who have undertaken congregational analysis have looked at the reasons why church members are drawn to particular churches. Most of us, it would seem, are attracted to communities of worship that have an established or emerging ethos with which we identify. Church communities have a distinct nature, they tell us, with which we also have a particular affinity.[8] So while we might like a church because of its worship style, or nearness, or commitment to young people, or because it is warm in winter, there is also something about its nature with which we implicitly identify. It might be a distinct 'family' church, where everyone knows everyone else and might be identified in family relationship terms. Or it might be a type of church that finds its identity in the causes and needs of the local community in which it is set. Whatever it is, somehow the church connects with something within our own life story.[9]

If this analysis is correct, then it is no real surprise to find the levels of support among these congregations for their clergy, since they will most likely be church communities that already embrace a distinct ethos of Christian liberalism. This survey does not pretend to suggest that there is support across the entire Church spectrum. There is not. This is probably best illustrated when we observe the varying positions of the wider Church leadership. How do the bishops of the Church deal with it?

The House of Bishops of the Church of England have come in for a good deal of criticism in the adoption of their 'official' position. Indeed, much of it might be well justified, for having created a document for discussion in the Church, *Issues in Human Sexuality* was offered rather less for discussion than might have been hoped, and for some seemed to act as a wall for the House to hide behind.

However, what this research threw up was a greater degree of understanding by some bishops of the complexities of the 'official' position as opposed to the pastoral situation in reality. Those bishops perceived to be furthest away from the grass roots (the diocesan bishops and primates) had seemingly the most ambiguous attitudes, whereas many of the suffragan or area bishops and the archdeacons appeared positively helpful. This perhaps endorses the view that there really is no substitute for first-hand experience. Many of the clergy applauded their senior pastors for at least trying to face the reality of the situation.

My working relationship with the archdeacon is very good. He has been extremely supportive here. The local bishop is supportive although he clearly finds it embarrassing to talk about. The diocesan bishop has made it quite clear that he cannot know anything about my private life.

Male priest with partner 6 years

When the new area bishop came to talk to me pastorally, he did ask about my support structures and I said that I had a particular friend. There was no comment. It was just noted.

Male priest with partner 1 year

The old bishop who put us in here was fantastic. He wanted to put a middle-class gay couple into a middle-class suburban parish like this. How we will get on with the new bishop I really don't know. The suffragan bishop has always been supportive and we get on well.

Male priest with partner 20 years

What the clergy and their partners had greatest difficulty with was the lack of consistency they encountered when they were trying to have a pastoral relationship on the one hand while wanting to be open and honest about who they were and what it meant to them. While there is a genuine desire to preserve demonstrable collegiality in supporting the sentiments outlined in *Issues in Human Sexuality*, it was clear that for many it was, in any practical sense, impossible to uphold. Some would speak the language of support for the document and then want to have an open dialogue with their gay or lesbian clergy, and this was often confusing for the clergy concerned. How should they respond?

My ordaining bishop was very supportive though he was tough and gave me quite a grilling at an interview I had in his office before I went to a selection conference. It was a tough interview, which lasted about half an hour. He raised some awkward questions but we covered a lot of ground. He was very supportive of my partner who had driven me over to the bishop's offices. He had waited in the car park for me and at the end of the interview the bishop actually told us both off because he had not gone into the office to wait for me.

Male priest with partner 20 years

Other clergy made what they felt were genuine attempts to make life easier for their senior pastors by being open about their situation, to avoid potential embarrassment. One rural dean described hosting a party for the clergy chapter at which the bishop was to be present. Since his partner was co-host with him and it would be the first time he had met the bishop, the rural dean thought it best to be open about his partner and avoid an awkward situation.

My partner was going to be there and I didn't want the bishop to find himself faced with someone and not knowing who it was and then having to be introduced. So to avoid putting the bishop in that situation, I thought I would have a friendly chat initially. The next day a senior assistant to the bishop called to tick me off. The bishop had said that he couldn't have that conversation with me. But when I met him a week or so later at another official event, both the bishop and his wife thanked my partner for our hospitality.

What became clear was that both men saw how bizarre the situation had become. Both were priests of integrity, living in an awkward situation in which they were attempting to meet each other and be loyal to other parties: the bishop to the House of Bishops and their position on gay relationships, and the dean to his partner. At that later meeting they were able to acknowledge that to each other.

We had a subsequent conversation where he shared the problems of being a bishop and I shared the problems of being gay clergy. I'm glad I did it, though I felt rotten at the time . . . as usual.

Male priest with partner 8 years

What is depressing about a statement like *Issues in Human Sexuality* is that if it becomes a policy statement, as many have now adopted it as, then it exposes itself to ridicule when its declarations are put into practice. Clergy, many of whom have been in partnerships for far longer than the statement has been in existence, are left uncertain as to how to relate to their bishop. Either it invites lies and deceit in which both bishop and priest are colluders, or if openness and honesty are adopted, the reward seems to be punitive action.

> *Where I was living the bishop found it extremely difficult because I was very direct with him about living in relationship and being sexually active. I wasn't prepared to go on constructing a tissue of lies and agreements that didn't bear any relation to reality. He then would not give me permission to officiate within the diocese. It was very distressing to no longer feel welcome in the diocese as a person of good standing and whose ministry was valid and wanted.*

> *Male priest with partner 5 years*

The primary relationship between bishop and clergy is really critical to the formation of any ministry. The priest is supposed to act on behalf of the bishop and they share the care of souls. Yet there is often this fundamental uncertainty as to how far they can trust each other.

> *I worry about how my bishop and archdeacon would react, but have tried to be as open as I can given the situation. At my institution, my partner sat beside me in the front row and so you think they would have been very foolish not to have worked out who we are for each other.*

> *Male priest with partner 15 years*

The search for meaningful commitment is not helped by a continued sense of uncertainty. It is a degrading and humiliating state for adult men and women to find themselves in.

The experiences of two women in the sample are particularly poignant. They both point to the culture context of the Church. It is still predominantly male, especially its leadership, and this has set the tone for discussion on homophile relationships, be they gay or lesbian. It is not an entirely male perspective that has prevailed, but it is not far from that. The failure to set the discussion within the parameters of loving and faithful partnerships and instead to launch out into a whirlpool of emotive language preoccupied with homosexual acts is most enlightening. The obsession of heterosexual masculinity fixes its attention on genital sex and its particular fearful horror, which it translates as revulsion, at the thought of anal intercourse. The lesbian women revealed this obsession for what it is.

> *My suffragan bishop wanted to be sure that I considered this to be a life-long relationship before he took it seriously. That was fair enough. My Director of Ordinands was very happy that I was in a stable, committed relationship which supported me through the process.*
>
> *Female ordinand with partner 1 year*

It would seem that in the male hierarchical world, the love of lesbian women for each other is viewed differently from the love that gay men have for each other. All the women in the sample endorsed this view to some degree. Their line managers (all men) were supportive of their relationships. They didn't seem to raise the same questions. Why?

> *I have never told any lies and wouldn't want to start now, but I haven't been asked the question since I went through the process of selection for ordination training. I think that women candidates are rather lucky in that it seems to be the case that they get asked the question about their sexuality rather less than men. It always seems to be assumed that you have not yet found the right man, or whatever.*
>
> *Female priest with partner 3 years*

The men assume that women are simply waiting for the right man! So not only is a lesbian relationship unthreatening because it doesn't venture into genital anal intercourse, it usually doesn't even get recognized in a predominantly male view of the world; single women are just unlucky that no man has yet found them.

The very worst of this is that the unique insights that lesbian women bring to our understanding of living in partnership never then get the hearing they deserve. Insights into tenderness, affection and friendship, which many described as essentials in their intimate relationships, get put aside. Facets of priesthood which manifest themselves in empathy, listening, compassion and an ability to stay with the pain of difficult circumstances, qualities that many men are wholly redundant of, are found in abundance in women, and in what women clergy in particular are able to bring to the Church's ministry. What a loss. All this comes about because we are unable to see that in sexuality and theology we are restricted by an overwhelmingly lop-sided perspective in the shape of heterosexual masculinity.

Belonging and believing

Belonging to the Church and believing in it despite the feeling of travelling second-class much of the time, was a prevailing theme from the outset for these clergy and their partners. Ironically, it was the very things that they found failing within the institution that they served that many found supplemented in their relationships. When they spoke of the significant partnerships that sustained them in their lives and ministries, many found themselves adopting a language of faith and community. It was in marked contrast to the sense of anxiety at one level and uncertainty at another of co-existing in a pastoral relationship that was determined by a statement that only highlighted how divided opinion was on same-sex partnerships, and how stultifying were its proposals for the clergy. What they lived at home set the pattern for what they found in ministry and was inspiring.

No gay or lesbian priest looks to live openly in a partnership because it is an easy option. On the contrary, while they may be aware of the love and support of the communities around them, they know too that there is a real sense of hostility in other parts of the Church nationally and worldwide. For many they remain objects of fear and loathing, despite the calls at every level for acceptance and communion. What keeps them in such a place as the Church?

One priest described his sense of vocation to priesthood as

enhanced by the love that sustained him in his partnership. He and his partner had been together for more than 15 years, but had only lived under the same roof for half of that time, out of consideration for the feelings of others. Having brought their relationship to a critical point, he realized that this was not simply about the feelings of others, but part of his vocation. He did not feel called to celibacy, but called to live openly with this man he had known and shared his deepest thoughts and affections with for more than seven years. Once he saw the relationship as a calling from God, it changed his and their entire approach. A calling required a testing out and a response. When we categorize and judge gay and lesbian partnerships, we might do well to ask the vocational question of what God is calling them, and all of us, into?

> *The longer we live together, the more we discover about each other and that discovery about each other is often like an 'ex nihilo' experience. Until the other person recognizes something in you, I may not have seen that in myself and in that sense it is a kind of ongoing learning. It is therefore an ongoing sense of greater identity.*
>
> *Male priest with partner 15 years*

In the creation narratives, God creates *ex nihilo*, that is, out of nothing. God creates by word, by command in Genesis; therefore God calls creation out and into being. The calling is something that Christians have reckoned to be participants in. God calls and we participate by responding to the call. The daring suggestion here is, of course, that God calls the gay man and lesbian woman not only to participate in the ongoing stewarding of creation, but to participate in and through the affection and intimacy of the relationships that they form. What gay and lesbian clergy do is to challenge the hitherto received tradition that this only happens to heterosexual men and women. If our relationships, in the language of faith, are forged as a response to the call of God, dare we think the unthinkable, that gay and lesbian partnerships are called out by God, and as such have important insights and things to say to the rest of creation?

Vocation demands discernment. The suggestion of a calling from

God demands that we rethink who we are in relation to God and what is being asked of us; what we are being called into. It is part of the discovery of who we are and what we will be. The same priest continues:

> In terms of faith, I think that self identity is all tied up with faith identity and becoming who I am is, after all, one of St Paul's great ethical injunctions. I think that I have discovered not only a great deal of who I am, but also of the meaning of love in this context. I find it difficult not to think about faith through the lens of my experience of having had a relationship, in the same way that I can't think about faith without thinking about relationships in church. God in the abstract doesn't mean a great deal to me.

Male priest with partner 15 years

So does God call us out through the gift of relationship? Is that restricted to those outside the ordained ministry? Might it not be time to rethink all this?

Whatever God calls each of us out of and into, it is seldom into a life of solitude and never one of isolation in loneliness. Even those called to hermetic life are held within the wider communion of saints, a mystical network of prayer that wraps itself around the world. There is something deeply sacramental about a relationship of intimate love. It conveys a sense of grace that is inexplicable yet observable to those who stand on its edges. Friends and neighbours, family and work colleagues often notice. We are different in love. Not simply more bearable, or easier to get along with in the workplace, but often a radiance or confidence will be described. We all benefit. Intimate relationships affect communities and enhance them. Clergy described their partnerships as such.

> At one time I was interested in monasticism and issues of models of holy living. I knew that I couldn't take vows of celibacy and so I tried to see my life with my partner as life in community. Sometimes it is really frustrating and sometimes it is a joy and there is God in the two of those things. It grounds me in the reality of what it means to live in community.

Male priest with partner 8 years

Some clergy partners described a sense of relief in this discovery; for in it their communities were served the better for it.

> There is something about belonging together that illuminates oneself. I find that in prayer particularly for some reason. I don't understand why or how, but somehow it does. What I see in him as our relationship has grown and developed is that whereas he used to be quite separate and distinct and tightly bounded, that has unravelled in a very positive sense. I see that not just in our relationship but in his relationship with the congregation and the family or whatever.
>
> *Partner to male priest 5 years*

If this is so then the call to live in community surely doesn't mean living in secrecy. What gay and lesbian partners seem to want in being 'out' is not the strident confrontational dimension that appears to be the hallmark of pressure groups like Outrage, but the simple desire to be known, acknowledged and accepted by the communities in which they live and serve. When the rest of us takes the trouble to look at what the heterosexual world readily takes for granted (holding hands in the street, a kiss hello or goodbye in public), is this really so very much to ask for?

It is not good to be alone

Gay and lesbian couples, like anyone else in the search for meaningful commitment, often find that their starting point has been loneliness. It is out of their sense of being alone that they appreciate the significant advantages of being in communion with another. For many this resonates strongly with how they understand the purposes of creation. In the second creation story of Genesis, God declares that it is not good that man, the pinnacle of his creation, should be alone and the entire rest of creation is brought forward for the man to name and identify. Meaningful partnership is discovered in the desire to share.

I think that there is a point in that, because I think that it means sharing things. It means taking you out of yourself occasionally. It means that you can see yourself occasionally through a different way. It can bring comfort. In the book of Ecclesiastes there are some interesting verses. It says that a man should not lie alone, but lie together with, interestingly, his friend, the two of them together to give each other warmth. And people do. Warmth is a key value in an intimate relationship with another person.

Male priest with partner 1 year

Sharing that warmth has for many couples brought healing from the hurts of a society and Church that has for so long left them with a real sense of exclusion and unwantedness. The sense of belonging to another is both comforting and challenging. The place of warmth is the place of safety and acceptance. The company of one who can be trusted in an uncertain wider environment is that place of warmth. But we need to remember that the word comfort in its original sense doesn't mean soft and gentle, more the opposite. In the great tapestry at Bayeux, there is an example of this in one of the panels. William the Conquerer is losing the Battle of Hastings and some of his soldiers are slinking away. The picture shows William chasing after them, waving his sword, and the tapestry panel reads, 'King William comforts his troops.' Comfort in this sense is about strength and active encouragement. It is this which moves couples from the place of loneliness to the discovery of just who they really are.

Belonging together makes a big difference to me. It's partly to do with filling the void of loneliness, of working out who I am in relationship to someone else and knowing I am somebody. For me it comes from knowing I was gay and being terrified of it. Living with my partner has transformed all that into a holistic thing. I am learning to integrate more of myself as somebody who can love somebody of my own sex, who can create a pattern of life akin to marriage and that has become very powerful and important.

Male priest with partner 4 years

Two women clergy described this encouragement as a key component of their relationship in which they are able to challenge one another. Simply by living openly in the company of another means that you cannot hide from the less likeable parts of their personality. Loving the worst of another person brought them actively within the shade of God's love and they understood that love. Their love for each other was somehow an icon of God's love. Recognizing that the defining of an intimate relationship and the decision to live that out in a committed and open way set them on a journey, and that journey brought to consciousness their understanding of a Christian spirituality. To love and be loved, warts and all, was to love as Christ.

For others this only emerged because of what they had found with this particular partner. It was unique to this relationship.

> I think that I feel more fully myself in relationship with her, because she brings things out in me that are not brought out in other ways.

> But identity is also about fully giving your self and therefore fully being yourself.

Female priests together 2 years

> I think that because of what has happened to me over the past year, my sense of what it means to be a gay woman in the Church has really been sharpened up. From the outset I was in no doubt that God was offering me something in this relationship and I wanted to take what I knew was a risk because I felt that it would be a tremendous opportunity to grow, having my heart opened and learning about loving and giving. I knew God was there from the beginning and it has deepened my sense of God as love.

Female ordinand with partner 1 year

One woman described how she found that being a priest means living on the edges of other people's lives. Often priests are perceived as 'not quite like other people', living their lives differently, committed to a daily routine of open prayer and public worship. In pastoral ministry they encounter others at times of crisis: death, sickness, rejection, imprisonment and so on. Most people don't do that in their day-to-day living. There is a sense in which people 'circle around' the clergy, giving them a wide birth most of the time, but glad of them in those acute moments. For this woman the priestly ministry was built on this uncomfortable place she described as the edge. She had experienced this both as a woman and as a gay woman, and it was an insight she had come to value.

> *Some of that is, for me, about the nature of priesthood being on the boundary in that liminal space. Being gay is another dimension of that. All those things feed together into a sense of who I am, how I minister, whom I minister to and what ministry is about. I think that being a couple enables us to do that jointly.*

> *Yes. We build on each other's strengths and experiences and we do talk a lot without breaking the bounds of confidentiality. I think that helps us both.*

> *Female priest and partner, together 2 years*

Other women spoke of a priesthood that had been shaped within a Church that had a lifelong history of being governed by men and whose theology reflected that. Until recently the ordained priesthood was the sole preserve of male culture and the resistance to the admission of women to holy orders seemed only to compound an already advanced sense of unwantedness within the Church. This clearly contrasted with the strong sense of calling felt from God. Yet this God was described in all liturgical language as male, and seemed to be represented only by men, who were actually a minority of the entire Church membership. The ordination of women to the priesthood was undoubtedly a major breakthrough, and the Church is still working through the effects of enabling that to happen. But for some there was a real cost to it all.

> *When I first met her, I was really angry with God and I found God's maleness and the patriarchy of the Church all too much. I stopped going to church. It was my partner who helped me heal from all those open wounds, and if I*

hadn't healed from them then I don't think I could have found God again. Instead I have found the motherhood of God and the loving nature of God, which I hadn't fully encountered until this crisis. It certainly deepened my faith and I couldn't have done it without her.

Female priest with partner 13 years

Her faith is deepened and she finds a greater understanding of priesthood in the now well-worked image of the wounded healer.[10] When she reflects upon the experience, she realizes that in order to be healed she had to re-enter it, before emerging with the insights she has gained not only of how God can be transforming, but of how God too can be transformed in the way we think and speak. This priest finds a place of comfort and security in a loving relationship that gives her the space to challenge the received perceptions of God and the descriptive language that accompanies it. From her experience she is empowered to find a new way of living faith and understanding priesthood in the motherhood of God.

The search for meaningful commitment has led most of our couples to a better place. Finding someone with whom to share life has been for most an enrichment of that life and has provided a more purposeful understanding of what it means to be a priest in the Church of God. Having ended the search, the journey of living begins. How does the gay and lesbian priest manage such a life? In the next chapter we will see.

Notes

1 *Issues in Human Sexuality*, 5:6, pp. 41–2.
2 *Issues in Human Sexuality*, p. 41.
3 *Issues in Human Sexuality*, 5:14, pp. 44–5.
4 *Issues in Human Sexuality*, 5:19, p. 46.
5 *Issues in Human Sexuality*, 5:15, p. 45.
6 James B. Nelson, *Embodiment*, Augsburg, 1979, p. 208.
7 Adrian Thatcher, *Living Together and Christian Ethics*, Cambridge University Press, 2002.
8 James F. Hopewell, *Congregation – Stories and Structure*, Fortress, 1987.

9 Penny Edgell Becker, *Congregations in Conflict: Cultural Models of Religious Life*, Cambridge University Press, 1999.
10 Alistair V. Campbell, *Rediscovering Pastoral Care*, Darton, Longman and Todd, 1981, pp. 37ff.

4

For better or worse

FROM COMMITMENT TO COMMUNITY

I remember somebody once telling me that being married was much nicer than getting married. A gross oversimplification, perhaps, but as a pastoral soundbite I frequently make use of it when preparing couples for a marriage ceremony. As the preparations are advancing, couples often feel that the wedding is being taken over by the interests of the family or the guests who are to be invited. The couple wonder for whose benefit they have embarked upon the day. I find myself telling them that I am sure that all will work out well for the day of the ceremony, and I am actually more interested in how they are to live from the day after the wedding ceremony.

Most gay and lesbian couples do not have the luxury of a marriage or other form of legal commitment ceremony. Only recently has it become lawful for such ceremonies to take place in certain parts of North America and Canada. In the United Kingdom, although legislation exists to give greater protection to gay and lesbian partners, and it is possible to register that partnership and mark it with a 'Do It Yourself' ceremony, there is nothing enshrined in the civil constitution to mark it legally – yet. The same is the case for the Church. Liturgical celebrations exist only at local level, and often in secret.

For many gay and lesbian couples this means that the opportunities to be open about their commitment are fewer. For clergy in such partnerships that is particularly so since they are acutely aware of the sensitivities of the wider Church in which they are active and committed. This Church is unresolved on how to relate to this significant proportion of its membership and pastoral leadership. Gay and lesbian clergy sometimes complain that they feel that they are talked about rather than talked to. They have become a subject for discussion rather than recognized as real people.

The reality is that there are a significant number of clergy who already live in committed partnerships that give purpose and fulfilment to their lives. Many of those partnerships, as we have seen, are quite long-standing, while others are still in formation, but all attest to their importance and worth in a wider Church climate that does not acknowledge them or offer public support. This means in effect that the relationship to which they have committed themselves becomes even more important in providing for these areas of need in the life of the clergy concerned.

The clergy described a sea change in their personal thinking and attitude to life when they decided to commit themselves to another. The benefits were very clear to them. There was a move away from the loneliness of living in isolation that was debilitating and sometimes dehumanizing. Some remembered compensating for the lack of companionable love by spending time away from the parish in a gay-friendly place that was quite unrelated to the rest of their life.

I feel much more settled and complete. I feel that I have a foundation that is being built in terms of a relationship that enables me to work much more happily. I don't do the clubs any more because this relationship strengthens the way that I live.

Male priest with partner 1 year

Others immersed themselves in more religion- or church-related activity, feeling that it was not possible to create any place that felt like home while they were on their own.

Christmas for me as a celibate meant religion, and I used to put up a six-inch Christmas tree on top of my telly for the servers' party which I had after Christmas. But I didn't do anything because I didn't have a home. I had places where I lived so that I could go out to work, but not a home. Now I have that home and a family and it is a joy. And that's about being embodied and incarnate.

Male priest with partner 5 years

This sense of 'home' was an important theme for others too. It was not simply about sharing a house. Home was another person; someone with warmth and with whom they felt welcomed.

> There is a person there to welcome me back when I arrive, or I am there to welcome him when he arrives. In all the things we do together, what makes it good is the sense in which I am able to do it all in consultation with him.

Male priest with partner 6 years

> That we can begin and end the day is quite important. Home is the fact of our being together, not simply the place or the location. When I go home to my partner, it is not the house that I go home to, it is her that I go home to. This being together is important.

Female priest with partner 3 years

Others recognized that there was a fine line between their dedication to the high sense of calling and ministry, and the need to hide within their working relationships to compensate for the personal empty times. Many had a pastoral ministry in which they engaged with the loneliness of others in regular visiting, only to go home and be alone themselves.

> I think that generally I am a much happier person now than the one who lived alone. I realize that particularly in those years of living and working as a priest by myself that I had a tremendous capacity to be a workaholic. There is a kind of selfishness about being a workaholic that I hadn't really realized until I started doing it. Now, having to deal with another person, and living the way we do now, I think I have become less selfish.

Male priest with partner 15 years

> I was lonely. I was extremely lonely. I don't think that anything you experience in theological training can prepare you for how lonely this job is. I know that I chose to come here and I have colleagues that I get on really well with, but at the end of the day there is no natural peer group and I had moved away from everybody that I knew. It was tough. Now I am part of her life and she is part

of mine, along with her friends and family, and so being part of the ebb and
flow of a community is rooted in a place for me now.

Female priest with partner 2 years

Economically, for most, living together made good sense too. Apart
from the few whose partners' pay was as modest as their own, nearly
everyone was enjoying a better standard of living from a financial
perspective. For those who had undertaken parental responsibilities
as well, this was particularly welcome.

The disadvantages to living openly in partnership were out-
weighed by the advantages, but were nonetheless there. Often these
problems were not so much related to any difficulty in the relationship to each other, as to the uncertainty with which the couple felt
they were perceived by their churches and communities. There was
frustration in this uncertainty.

One certain disadvantage is that because we are living an open life, but not yet
fully open life, I think it is quite hard for people to know, for example, who to
invite to dinner; whether they are inviting me or whether they are inviting both
of us. Often what happens is, I might get invited out for dinner and there will
be no mention of him at the time. Then later on I will get a phone call asking
me whether I am vegetarian and they will slip in to the conversation the ques-
tion, 'Is he coming as well?' So, it is like they know but they don't want to
offend in any way. It is done with the best of intentions but it can be quite awk-
ward sometimes.

Male priest with partner 15 years

For some the uncertainty fuelled an anxiety as to how they should
present themselves as a couple at a social gathering with people they
didn't know. The desire to be open had to be balanced by the desire to
be accepted hospitably not just by their host, but by the wider circle
the host may have gathered.

When I get invited out, who are they inviting? Sometimes they do say you and
your partner, but then what if we go and discover that a whole lot of bigoted

Christians are there too and they are disapproving? You think, are they going to write letters? It is just not clear!

It's that thing about if we're at an event and someone comes up to speak to me. Normally you would say 'Hello, I'm such-and-such's partner, and that's why I'm here.' But I can't do that. I have to be cautious, for his sake not mine.'

Male priest and partner 6 years

Most agreed that finding time for each other was something that needed to be monitored. It was easy to drift into the all-consuming work mode and those who were unable to live together all the time expressed a great need for organization of time and good communication.

We have both least enjoyed getting up at 5 a.m. on a Monday morning to drive home. The need to adjust on Friday evening too, by that I mean changing from being alone to opening up in front of someone after the solitary nature of the week.

Female ordinand with partner 1 year

It is how we organize our time. There are days when we just don't see each other. I go off to work at 7 a.m. and when I get back she could be going off to a meeting and it might be 9.30 p.m. before we actually meet.

There are no children for us to consider and for me, I am one of those people for whom work is play. I would always choose to do the work thing and she is very good at stopping that. She is probably one of the big factors in my not being burned out in the time I have been here.

Female priest and partner 2 years

Thinking about someone else does take a lot of getting used to and in a sense I have to bring myself up and remind myself of these things. It would be so easy to slip back into self-centredness.

Male ordinand with partner 8 years

74

Companion, communion and trinity

Miss Nichols died recently. She was 93 and had long since stopped coming to church, her body dictating that she could no longer manage the steep hill. She received communion at home, and these visits were occasions that she and I would both look forward to, not only for our time of prayer and communion, but for the bright conversation that ensued. Despite being brought up in the tradition in which home communion should see me leave the communicant saying their prayers, to return on another occasion for a social visit, I have never found anyone who understood the logic of this. So now I don't, and with Miss Nichols it made the best sense. For more than 40 years she had shared her home with Miss Cooper, who had died when Miss Nichols was 80, and for the last 13 years she had grieved the passing of someone her friends and neighbours referred to politely as her 'companion'.

Companion is one of those words associated with the world of gentlefolk and because of this it has lost the power of its derivative sense. It has come to mean a long-standing platonic friendship, usually between two persons of the same sex, who might share a house together, but not a bed. There is faithfulness and fondness, but there is definitely no hanky-panky after dark. It is for the mature person and not for youth. All of this may be true but this description neglects one important dimension. The word companion derives from two words, meaning 'together' and 'bread'. A companion is therefore one with whom we share bread, or break bread. It is a daily basic undertaking of sharing food, but with the undertone that this providing and sharing food is a sign of a particular commitment. Christians especially should need no convincing of this when they participate in eucharistic worship and in particular the receiving of the Holy Communion. It is an intimate moment created in a public forum, a mark of our committed relationship with God and of God's loving faithfulness to us.

It was this kind of intimacy that marked the nature of the relationship between Miss Nichols and Miss Cooper. This became increasingly clear to me, the more Miss Nichols spoke about her. Her recollections were of holidays together and of one with whom she could share her deepest thoughts. The manner in which she spoke of her passing was one of lament. When Miss Nichols died, her executor advised me that she had left explicit instructions that she should be buried with Miss Cooper. Years before, they had together bought a double plot at the cemetery. It was abundantly clear that these two women had loved each other all that time. Theirs had been a companionship in which, inwardly, two lives had been broken open each day as they shared bread, while outwardly it suited their friends and neighbours to see them as a couple of old dears who shared a house.

Miss Nichols often described her life with Miss Cooper as a gift. She had never expected to meet her and always maintained that her life would have been the poorer without her. What does it mean to see an intimate relationship as a gift from God? Most of those who shared insights from their partnerships maintained that it was a gift, and by that gift their relationship enhanced their faith and sense of living in the midst of God. For many it allowed them to think more broadly about God and how God might live for them.

> I started life in a very proper, born-again evangelical household, thinking that my sexuality was a total curse and wondering how I was ever going to live with it. I even thought that it would probably have been a jolly sight better if I had just quietly died. So it has taken me a long time – I'm now 57 – to come to consider my sexuality, and therefore our relationship and our home and all the rest of the things we do together, as a gift from God, which I now do. It has taken quite a lot of work and thought, but our life together is a gift and I am very thankful to God for it.

> Male priest with partner 20 years

This is an interesting and challenging insight from a couple who have spent much of their life hearing the Church describe their relationship generally, and their sexual expression of it specifically, as a sin. There was evidence to show that many had suffered years of denial and repression, the agony of which had only been healed in the formation of a loving partnership. One described the unhappiness of this self-loathing and how the discovery of God in the phenomenon of perfect love had rescued him from it.

I must admit that from my upbringing in the Church, where what I am was simply seen as a bad thing, it took an age to come to terms with myself and getting over all this. It's a kind of internalized homophobia that I think a lot of gay people have. What I have found is that understanding God as love has helped me face all that. Where that love expresses itself as supporting and affirming and a good thing, there God is. I don't see how that can be bad.

Male partner to priest 23 years

Others felt the same. Theirs had been a journey into discovering the generosity of God's love and seeing it mirrored in the relationship that had happened for them. It was a welcome respite from the personal fear of repression and the institutional condemnation they felt from some quarters of the Church. But it had been more. Like many of us, the couples taking part had never really taken the time to reflect on how their most significant relationship informed and influenced the way they thought about God and how they passed that on to the people that they ministered among. Yet when they took that time, it was clear that the fruit of that partnership held for them the very signs that they found when they described God as they perceived him in scripture, and as handed on in the traditions of the Church and in their own experience.

Discovering God through the relationships described in scripture alone was agreed to be a very complex thing. The ancient Hebrew Scriptures describe what would be some very complicated human relationships, if we took them literally and tried to use them in our attempts to order our lives. It is untenable and irresponsible to argue sensibly for or against same-sex relationships simply on the grounds of what scripture tells us about them. Certainly there is condemnation of sexual practice that is abusive to the laws of hospitality, but if we take a general overview of some of the principal relationships of attraction and marriage, a very complex picture emerges.

In much of contemporary Jewish culture, and large sections of

Christian culture, great importance is placed on finding a life partner who shares the same faith principles. Yet much of ancient scripture gives us a picture of cultural diversity, heterosexual polygamy and physical attraction across the spectrum. In Genesis, Jacob has relations with four different women, and although there is some sort of betrothal they are not wives as we understand it, because there is no marriage. He has children by all of them. Joseph is presented to us as a very popular and attractive man. Pharaoh finds him attractive, Potiphar finds him attractive, and Potiphar's wife finds him attractive. Joseph rebuffs her advances, but eventually ends up with an Egyptian wife and gives his blessing to the sons of that union. This is confusing imagery if we are looking for support for the common faith principles of a one-to-one heterosexual life partnership. Yet scripture does not balk at life as it really is.

> The texts we read week by week tell us about all sorts of people getting together. It does not offer us anything looking like traditional monogamy. It has polygamy. It has people who are passionate about one person and then passionate about another person. It has Jacob who wants one sister but then gets the other. It gives us David, who is loved by one particular man and then marries his sister Michal in what proves to be a very unhappy relationship. She loved David, but he didn't love her in return. He loved her brother.

> *Male priest with partner 2 years*

There are instances of human darkness in relationships. Rebecca plots to deceive Isaac and steal the birthright from Esau. Is this a good model of intimate relationship? Sarah drives out Hagar, which is very cruel. Tamar disguises herself as a prostitute to deceive Judah, her father-in-law, to become pregnant by him. The story of the daughters of Lot is extreme and grotesque if we read it at face value. There is not much to be gleaned about tender, trusting, faithful relationships here, though perhaps something can be learned about the importance of lineage and biological continuity and the vulnerability of women driven to desperate acts in a world where men govern and upon whom they depend for everything.

This is a story that flies in the face of everything depicted as conventional sexual morality, which we are told is what the Bible stands for. But it just doesn't! What we have are very passionate and complicated interactions in the sexual context. These are passionate and complicated people.

Male priest with partner 2 years

Passionate and complicated interactions they may be, but also very open and explicit ones. There is no sense of deliberately hiding things away in the stories of ancient scripture, and the things that are hidden are continually being unearthed by scholars. It is the task of academics to find new ways of looking at things, and the recent gifts of Biblical criticism, contextual analysis and social and sexual perspective have all contributed to this. But they are gifts, and the gifts of intellectual insight are only fully appreciated when they are received – rather like the gift of human relationship.

Gifts are also only fully appreciated if we are prepared to open them! The relationships described in scripture are best appreciated in that way. What we have is quite often a messy record of human interactivity, not always understood, either at the time or subsequently, but nonetheless an honest record of human experience. These experiences are set within a life context of a struggle to know and understand what it means to live within the creative love of God. Where these stories contrast starkly with much of our contemporary human experience within the Church is in their bare-faced honesty. They are an untidy mess. In the contemporary Church we spend far too much time closing down this kind of openness, and have been the poorer for it.

This culture of cloaking the open truth is not the unique possession of the institutional Church and those who are prone to criticize the Church's leaders might like to stop and think before they do so. Stephen Law, who teaches philosophy at Heythrop College in the University of London, has written some fun and accessible work on this issue.[1] Law points out that in western philosophy there are, broadly speaking, two contrasting views of truth-telling. The first, espoused by Immanuel Kant, is an absolutist view. Kant advocated that morality took strict and absolute imperatives. Do not kill, do not steal, do not lie, etc. would be examples of this principle, over which there is no exception. The other is the view of the philosopher John Stuart Mill. His was a utilitarian view. He deemed that human beings told the truth according to how they envisaged the consequences of their truth-telling – in other words, usually according to the happiest outcome. If your grandmother buys you the most ghastly birthday present and asks if you like it, you tell her that you do, because she will leave your birthday a happy woman.

The problem with the utilitarian view is that it is actually impossible to guess exactly what the consequences of your action will be. Yet this is the view the Church and its bishops have adopted towards their gay and lesbian clergy. They have assented to a 'truth' that is utilitarian, having tried to guess what the consequences will be and what is likely to keep the wider Church happy. What scripture does is the opposite, because it is rooted in human experience. It tells the story, regardless of the consequences, and leaves the legacy of tradition to work it out in the light of new knowledge and insight.

This is no different from the insights of those who are taking part in this work. Impatient with the shortcomings of the utilitarian or consequentialist view, they adopt an absolutist position, as the more honest one, which places human relationships back in the open, allows them to be seen as people rather than someone else's problem and resists the growing phenomenon of viewing them as an interesting subject for study under the social sciences lens.

All of this makes best sense in our understanding of God as Trinity and encountering God in the Eucharist. There is little point in wanting to live openly unless we are talking about being active participants in the life of the community. But where does that community begin?

One of the oldest definitions of what it means to be Church is found in the first letter of Paul to the Corinthians, chapter 12. The apostle describes the community of faith as a body. Each member is like a part of the body. It is different, and has different functions, responsibilities and even gifts. No one part is more important than any other, and all parts depend on each other's difference in order for

the entire body to function. Paul tells the Corinthians that they are to
see themselves as if they were Christ's very own body. Metaphoric-
ally, they live and act and function in the living out of Christ's gospel
as if they were that body itself. This sense of interdependence will
counter their previous revelling in independence and competition
that certain Corinthian Christians seem to have had with one
another.

So ideally we might say that our sense of community ought to
begin with our understanding of the Church itself as the body of
Christ. But clearly what we currently have is an imperfect mirror
image of that ideology. There are differences and factions within the
wider Church as we know it that some find intolerable. If the entire
baptized communion is considered to be included, it doesn't follow
that everyone feels that way. Among those who don't feel included
are its gay and lesbian members.

In June 2003 Dr Jeffrey John, Canon Theologian of Southwark
Cathedral and the prospective Bishop of Reading, was interviewed
for *The Times* newspaper about his 27-year relationship with another
priest. In the course of the interview Dr John outlined how he saw
that relationship and all relationships that claimed a Christian framework. They mirrored a sense of divine community that was best
expressed in the Christian understanding of the Trinity.

The mystery of love is in the end, the mystery of giving yourself
away. This week we are celebrating the feast of the Trinity, which is
all about God himself existing as a relationship of love in his own
nature. God is love. Love between persons who are individual and
yet given completely to the other, is a mystery that reflects God's
own nature.

People think the mystery of the trinity is strange, but it is not.
You find out in a good relationship, a good marriage, what it really
means to lose yourself in the other and somehow find your true self
in the process of giving yourself away to the other. That is what
the Church should be getting across to people. Finding out that fact
of experience is actually finding out something about the mystery
of God.[2]

I find these insights quite compelling and, for Western Christians who skip past the feast of the Trinity as if it were a mathematical embarrassment, it is a refreshing way of re-entering a theological mystery that evades us yearly, thanks to a thousand inept sermons trying to explain the trinity as three cricket stumps but one wicket, or ice, water and steam, three manifestations of the same wet substance. The churches of the East have no such problems. Their depiction of the trinity is more fluid and mirrors the relationship image. The term they use to describe the trinity is 'perichoresis', which could be interpreted as dancing in a circle. It is a wonderful image of interactivity in the gracefulness of movement and a fine depiction of what any committed relationship between human beings, attempting to reflect the love of God, might become. Those who are lucky enough to know what it is like to dance well with a partner, moving with graceful correspondence, will see the power of this image. It is a very creative image inspired by a very creative God.

> When we talked about this, we came very quickly to the same conclusion, which is that we believe ourselves to be loved by God and made by God the way that we are. So our image begins with God the creator and God of love, but then there is more than that. God the creator created with purpose for us in our lives, which is not separate or independent from everything else. So the God who made her fantastically patient and therefore a wonderful teacher, also made her gay and therefore my partner, and the two things are not in some kind of separate box.

> *Female priest with partner 2 years*

> I understand God as person in loving relationship, and as humanity created in that image it seems to me that we are created to be those who love and are loved in a sacrificial, self-giving way. It seems to me that it is probably only in an intimate relationship that you have with a loving partner that we can most fully express that love as human beings.

> *Female priest with partner 3 years*

When we describe something as graceful, we intend a picture of beauty in movement, which I think is a good way of describing a trinitarian perichoresis. God is on the move, but in a way that manifests God as beauty and harmonious interaction. Sometimes we speak of moments of grace as being like that, moments when, quite unexpectedly, we survey a scene or hear a story that strikes us in such a way that we can only look or listen in wonder and amazement. A friend of mine recalled, as a teenager, his father returning from the war. He had been invalided out and returned to his home village. He never walked again and spent the rest of his life in a wheelchair. But he forged a firm friendship with Mr Percival, who had been blinded in action. His father became Mr Percival's eyes and Mr Percival became his father's legs. Neither of them was cured, but there emerged, he said to me, an enormous healing as patience and compassion grew between them; two men, different in their needs, but finding fulfilment in each other. The two men became for my friend an icon of God's grace.

I would not want to make the mistaken assertion that gay couples simply find each other as incapacitated souls, needy and broken people, like the 'blind and the lame'. Gay and lesbian couples are probably no more needy than anyone else in seeking fulfilment in a loving relationship. What I am saying is that if moments of grace reveal themselves in the unexpected encounter, why are we continually surprised by it? What consistently emerged from the clergy in this survey was that the discovery of another person with whom they could imagine finding fulfilment was a grace-filled moment and something that propelled them into a creative ministry. Being loved and being allowed to love was indeed a healing thing, and not just for them and the person they became committed to. Because this affected their ministry as Christian men and women, they felt that the whole body of Christ had been served. The model of the trinity and living in loving relationship was the springboard to serving Christ more effectively in the Church.

For many of the couples, this moment had forced a rethink of how they understood God in the mission of the Church and their ministry. This is probably quite important since much of the current debate on gay and lesbian relationships has lamented how the issue has proved a distraction from the more pressing priorities of the Church, namely its mission and commitment to evangelism. These claims seem to be made by Christians who are not gay and who benefit from preserving the status quo, or by those who fail to see that unless the Church can deal with its own implicit nature, it will not be an effective vehicle for mission and outreach. The Church is people. People have bodies and relate to each other through them. Together, those bodies describe themselves as Christ's body, each different, but in need of the other. What most of those surveyed seemed to be saying was that being loved and being able to love clearly increased the possibility of a better quality of ministry, which in turn would enhance the Church's mission and outreach.

> *I am sure that this relationship has made an impact on my ministry simply because as a person who loves and is loved on a personal level I am a very much more fulfilled person than I might be. I think that while I don't suppose you need to experience everything in order to understand everyone else and how they feel, there are many situations in which the Christian minister will find his or her self in a situation where there may be no personal experience. That doesn't mean that you have no ministry in that situation. Having said that, as a partnered person I have an experience that I can relate to and that might help in some situations.*
>
> *Male ordinand with partner 7 years*

I have argued elsewhere that a commitment to reflective practice in a pastoral ministry of any kind is not simply a luxury that the minister should allow if time permits.[3] It is rather an essential dimension to good practice, in that it often not only allows the minister insights of self, but can allow enduring and helpful ways of seeing God emerge in the light of pastoral action. This in turn has the effect of enhancing future pastoral practice. We are fed by these insights and thus reminded that the ministry we commit ourselves to is not our own. For the Christian minister it can only make sense when located within the ministry of Christ. Christian ministry is done in the name of Christ and with the purpose of seeing Christ revealed in the agency of pastoral practice. Many of the participants found powerful images of God and Christ renewed in and through their relationships. Some found old images taking on a new and vibrant vitality for the first time because of them.

I think that I have learned more about the importance of honesty. I think I have always been quite a good listener and the thought of God as the one who hears has been an important theological image. But more than that, if God is honesty and truth, then I am learning to express with clarity and honesty my thoughts and feelings. My partner has taught me the priority of being above merely thinking and doing. Thinking and doing are more authentic now as an act of Christian witness because I am allowed to be more openly and honestly myself.

Male priest with partner 5 years

Being with this man has certainly made life better for me out there. My under-standing of God is of one who is inclusive of that which is otherwise excluded. I can think of how Jesus was forced into situations of stretching the bound-aries, which of course in one way led to his crucifixion. Our relationship has reminded me of the power of that and of its danger and costliness. So there is an 'edgeness' to being a gay priest in a committed partnership, but I think that, like other people, I owe it to the wider world and not least to the Church to be as open as I can and say that Church is not just the cosy club of conformity. Being a priest isn't a cosy thing to be. It's about living and working and being in that marginal place.

Male priest with partner 2 years

I think that the whole experience of being gay and in relationship in the Church has offered a number of experiences about being different, being out-siders, about being abnormal and to use theological language about being strangers in exile. All those theological motives have been important and the sense that because we have found support, love and care in the Church, we have also found liberation through faith. I feel as though I am in exile and being liberated at the same time. I never knew what it was to be accepted, which in theological language is the language of adoption and grace. I don't think I really knew what it meant until I met him.

Male priest with partner 15 years

85

Truth-teller, outsider and liberator

The perception of God as truth in the reflected experience of these couples leans heavily towards an absolutist view of truth as opposed to the utilitarian view, described earlier. Gay and lesbian clergy seem to be declaring that truth-telling based on the consequential outcome of any given situation within the Church is no longer satisfactory. There seems to be two reasons at least for this.

The first is that utilitarian truth-telling, though appearing more natural to human institutions, has a limited shelf-life. Whatever the outcome of utilitarian truth-telling, it is nonetheless partial. It will always remain challenged by the absolutist view. Utilitarian truth-telling is a human solution to a human problem. In the case of the Church it is deployed as a form of diplomacy to keep the peace and keep as many people on board the wobbly ship as possible. It has the effect of buying time, but it is always prone to renewed challenge in the wake of contextual change. We find examples of this in a review of the Church's stance on money-lending for interest, artificial contraception, second marriages in church after a divorce, and the ordination of women. What is perceived as manageable truth in one generation is reshaped when revisited in another.

The second is that an absolutist view of truth has more resonance with an understanding of God as revealed in scripture and, for Christians particularly, the Gospels. Gay and lesbian priests, hidden inside an institution held together by utilitarian truth-telling, have found a way of life that does not quite ring true with the Jesus of the Gospels that we all seek to emulate. There is a sense of frustration and discomfort at knowing there is something to tell and having to hold it back. The couples who have found love, comfort and support for their personal lives and often inspiration for their public ministries through these relationships have good news to tell and they are being told not to tell it. What they discover in reading the Gospels and locating their own lives within them is identification with God in Christ, who reveals that the search for truth is not utilitarian. In fact, quite the opposite. Absolute truth is hopelessly impractical and very costly, but it is essential to the whole ethos of God's Kingdom or God's

Reign, in which the social values, class systems and economic principles which govern human life are turned on their head. Taking this view of God as Truth seriously challenges not only the fact of their relationships, but also how they should be lived out.

I was settled and content being a single person working out my ministry and within six months I had to come to terms with a whole different way of being and I guess that was very good for that bit of me which thought I had got it sorted in a rather smug sort of way. It threw me and I had to face who I was within this community which is full of people living on the margins. And I began to identify with some of that in a new way.

From my point of view I had to stop being the sort of Christian who pays lip service to the notion of inclusion from the margins. It is not what I planned but it does seem to be an exciting and challenging way to live. I am not used to it but it is showing me a different way of living.

Female priest and partner 3 years

The search for God as Truth began for some of these couples by identifying Jesus of the Gospels as someone prepared to enter the social margins. This is not a new idea, but it is one that gay and lesbian couples, and in this instance clergy, have found themselves identifying with. Those who oppose any change in the Church's stance on its discipline regarding gay lifestyles tend to dismiss it as being part of a gay rights campaign and a liberal conspiracy. But if we set this viewpoint within a tradition that takes both scripture and experience seriously, the conspiracy theory is difficult to sustain.

To some extent we are all liberal, if we define the term from its source. As writers like Andrew Sullivan make clear, however, we live in an era, particularly within the Church where few will admit to a liberalizing tendency, when by skilful propaganda the term has been reduced to an insult, robbed of its authority and context. Liberalism is used to describe a banal form of puritanism, and itself whittled into marginality.[4] The term has come to be associated with those who advocate tolerance and a lack of prejudice, but this does little justice to the word. Liberal finds its root in the Latin word *liber*, which means free in the sense of not being held in slavery. From it we derive other words like liberty and liberation. These are terms far removed from any sense of tolerance. Who wants to spend their life being tolerated? And who can find a Gospel of Jesus the Tolerator? To tolerate something or someone does not require us to love them or even like them – something which I think even the most conservative reader of the Gospels would agree is absent from these accounts of Jesus and his ministry.

It is the commitment towards an authentic liberalism, which properly challenges power structures that cease to serve the underdog, that seems to characterize the ministry of Jesus. We cannot say that he lives in the margins – the Gospel narratives show clearly that his ministry took him back and forth across the boundaries of social and political difference – but he is clearly described as being prepared to enter the world of the socially excluded, economically oppressed and the ritually/religiously unclean. What we are dealing with in our contemporary application is an entire category of human life that not only *feels* excluded, but *is* excluded from, or at best tolerated by, a wider Church. In toleration love or liking barely exists. Gay and lesbian clergy are at last saying that they have had enough of being tolerated.

The change from toleration to affirmation is the movement from the place of exclusion and exile to that of full acceptance, understanding and embrace. To tolerate something or someone might, with some stretch of the imagination, get away with being described as an act *prompted* by love. Putting up with something or being patient about a situation or a person might be seen as an act of love, but at best it feels like love done at arm's length. It doesn't necessarily require engagement or close encounter that might actually change the self. It is not the same as liking something or someone, which has a definite sense of acceptance about it. If I like someone, there is usually, if not a sense of agreement or tacit approval, the feeling of comprehension and understanding.

The Catholic theologian James Alison helpfully makes this distinction in some of his work. In an essay called 'Confessions of a Former

Marginaholic', he recounts his experiences as a Dominican in South America.[5] Here he finds his life almost systematically stripped of what he had hitherto regarded as reasons for being at all. A teacher at the university, writing up his doctoral thesis, and a man in love with another man, he then seems to lose it all. The man he loves dies of AIDS, the ecclesial authorities conspire to remove him from his teaching position and eventually from his Order, and although his thesis is published as a useful work, he sees his motives for writing it in a different light. But all of this brings with it a new revelation.

> These then were the three factors which seemed to combine in my experience of dying: loss of ambition and the need to succeed, loss of a fake and compulsive life project, and transformation of a defining shame into something which holds neither fear or fascination, and with it the possibility of just being and liking being, human.[6]

This moves him along from the need to invite rejection and to look to live on the margins of life, and instead, like Paschal, redefines his understanding of God. Instead of perceiving God as one in the centre of the life we aspire to, with ourselves on the outside, Paschal describes God as a circle whose centre is everywhere and whose circumference is nowhere.[7] We can adopt this view, Alison says, because Christ is in the centre of every experience. For the Christian it is Jesus who occupies the place of marginalization and victimage, and because Christ does this and makes such places sacred and no longer to be feared, that centre is everywhere, including where you and I are. This understanding sets Alison free to see his life in an entirely different light.

> I seem to find a growing sense of being in the centre of what it is all about. And this is not a counterfactual claim to power, because it is not a claim at all. Rather it is a discovery of being given something which is also being given to someone exactly in the degree to which I am taking part in a huge, and largely hidden adventure.[8]

Because Christ transforms the margins of life from places and relationships of disdain and dislike to ones of acceptance and liking, we are both challenged and enabled to inhabit those same places, or at least live alongside those who inhabit them, namely those we so often pledge ourselves to tolerate, claim to love, but cannot bring ourselves to like. We are made to face our true selves and the possibility of being transformed by those very same relationships.

> I suggest that someone who is really aware of being liked . . . is able to defuse someone else's place of shame and make it spacious . . . Thus being able to share in something as equals becomes not a demand or a burdened place or a tortured will, but part of the discovery of who I am as I find myself being turned into something different by a spacious sharing with someone who I am like.[9]

Facing our true selves in the way that lays us open to the possibility of such change is a bold but necessary step. It forces us, first, to think about why we have an aversion to, dislike of, or even hatred towards certain things and people. In this instance, the gay and lesbian clergy in the survey are posing a challenge to those parts of the Church that find them so disagreeable or dislikable as to reject their existence outright or demand that they be seen and not heard. Loving the sinner and hating the sin would seem to be one of the most sanitized forms of camouflage that currently exists to prevent the fundamental question being asked, 'What is it about the very existence of gay men and lesbian women and the whole idea of feeling attracted to someone of the same sex as me that makes me react in this defensive and fearful way?'

I don't want to enter into a discussion here about why some people are homosexual and others not, or the degree to which one might be attracted to others of the same sex. I am not particularly concerned with biological condition, social influences, or the strength of a particular relationship with one parent or another, in determining how the homosexual character and make-up comes about. That has been done elsewhere and there is plenty to read on the matter. But I do want to share some of the experiences of acceptance and rejection

from gay and lesbian clergy and offer some insights into why the
model of God as liberator is such an important one for them.

The more senior clergy were able to describe the remarkable major
change in social attitudes generally. Couples with one or both partners in their retirement gave descriptions of rejection and fearful
hostility in the early years. Attitudes then mellowed as the whole gay
scene moved to a more open place in human consciousness.
Comments like this were not uncommon.

> My parents and my brother were hostile with a sort of studied indifference,
> choosing to think that if they just ignored it and said nothing it might go
> away.
>
> *Male priest with partner 32 years*

> I have experienced some hostility when my parents discovered that I was gay
> and insisted that I went for psychiatric help. It was after I told the pastor at my
> local church that I suppose word got out and people would literally cross the
> road to avoid speaking to me.

> Growing up where I did, I had to learn to be secretive about my sexuality even
> though there were some gay people in the provincial cathedral city where I
> lived. There was great pressure to conform and I did conform and I never really
> let on.
>
> *Male priest and partner together 20 years*

Apart from these examples of some (now quite elderly) parents finding it difficult to come to terms with a son or daughter who might be
gay or lesbian, most experienced levels of affirmation and acceptance
that surprised them, but for which they were very glad. At a local
level, friends and neighbours were non-judgemental and very warm
towards them. Most found similar attitudes within their local church
community, some even being asked regularly by young parents to
babysit. One couple were part of a team that offered daytime relief to
young parents (usually mothers) in their congregation, by taking
their children out to the park. Most were invited to local community

social events. One couple were sought out by their City Council to run a support and advice centre for gay and lesbian members of the local community. It was only in the wider Church community that the weight of repression was felt.

In terms of hostility, I do experience the Church as hostile to us. It doesn't even seem to understand human relationships very well, let alone ones not of a traditional cut. I can give you all sorts of examples of love and affirmation from individuals within the local church, but the machinery of the wider Church, the Big Message, if you like, is perpetually hostile.

For instance, lots of people in our diocese are predisposed to regarding our relationship as valid and licit; nonetheless they won't invite us explicitly to a diocesan party, or the bishop's reception or a deanery do. In that sense we remain invisible. It's like parents who teach their children the right things about loving everyone and not to differentiate on the basis of race, and then when their son or daughter comes home with a boy or girlfriend of a different colour and ethnicity to them, they can't deal with it.

Male priest and partner 8 years

What has happened to Jeffrey John in the whole Bishop of Reading thing feels like a personal rejection of me and my partner and the way we live our life even though they know nothing about me or us or Jeffrey either. I am not one of those who is easily moved to tears but I did find myself weepy when trying to talk about it to the other students on my course. I wondered whether I wanted to be ordained into a Church that behaves so badly. I have been pleasantly surprised at the reaction of the secular world, who don't seem to see it as a problem. It is the Church as usual which seems to be unprophetic, behind the times and bigoted – and gets away with it.

Female ordinand with partner 13 years

Others had experience of the Church in confusion, wanting to be supportive but unable to go beyond certain stages. One couple described how their bishop had placed them in a parish where local clergy were deemed to be supportive. What they found was support in theory, but difficulty turning that into a practical reality. They had to move. Another couple experienced similar confusion when making a move from one parish to another.

> I was offered a job in another diocese some years ago and by the time I got to the interview process, the people concerned had discovered, through other sources, that I was gay and that I had a partner, and they were very positive and affirming about that. It was explicitly talked about. We both went to dinner. Then when it came to the actual appointment, it was made on the understanding that we would not live together.
>
> Male priest with partner 15 years

There is an obvious lack of understanding as to what it means to live in a gay or lesbian partnership. It is clear that it is assumed that gratuitous sex is the sole criterion for establishing such partnerships. Numerous couples complained about this level of misunderstanding and the assumption that all same-sex attraction was shallow, promiscuous and insincere.

> The first example that comes to mind occurred while speaking at a meeting of a deanery synod. They asked me to address the meeting as a gay priest. At the end of the meeting a rather offensive man deemed it appropriate to raise all sorts of questions about buggery and anal intercourse, focusing entirely upon a repertoire of sexual activities. Acts rather than relationships.
>
> Male priest with partner 5 years

What is it about the human make-up that resolutely refuses to accord any space in the mind to the possibility of generous same-sex love, and simply accept it? I belong to a musical arts club with a substantial membership. Some of the most talented members are gay men. At one of the first meetings I attended, one of them played a piece of music quite brilliantly. The man sitting next to me complimented this and then added, 'But of course, he is gay, you know.' I replied that I didn't know but asked if this made any difference. My neighbour said that it didn't really, and he didn't mind gays at all so long as they kept themselves to themselves and didn't try anything on with him.

Herein lies a clue to the answer to this question. Ultimately there is fear. The fear is one of unknowing. Gay men and lesbian women are for the most part unrecognizable in their appearance as anything other than regular men and women. They are normal human beings and live normal lives. They do normal jobs, take normal holidays, get sick, get fed up, get hung over and get on with life. Basically, being gay is not as much of a problem for gay men and lesbian women as it is for those who are not gay, and men in particular who are often ill at ease with their bodies and able to describe themselves only in terms of what they are *not*, in relation to other people. So they have no problem with Lily Savage and John Inman because one is a cross-dresser and the other outrageously camp, and they only have to relate to them from the other side of a television screen. There is no real meeting point. But what if they found themselves getting on well with another man, enjoying his company – and then discovered him to be gay. It is all so normal, but then that one moment of realization changes normal to fearful. Why?

James Alison explores the themes of acceptance, normality and fear in *Faith Beyond Resentment*, a book on the Gerasene demoniac in the Gospel of Mark.[10] He notes that the response of the townspeople to the healing of Legion is that they were fearful and he asks what it is that makes them so. They hadn't been afraid when he was running around and bruising himself. They had been used to his differences, tearing his clothes and cutting his body. They could handle what they perceived as his madness or possession because it was so far removed from their own experience; it was simply something other than themselves and something they were not. What they couldn't cope with was seeing him clothed and in his right mind. As Alison reads the dynamic of this story, what had kept them in their right minds before was knowing that Legion was not in his right mind. Legion had some value for this community in his mad, demon-possessed way, but this has now evaporated. They have to think about him in a new way. They have to relate to him in a new way. No longer is his madness a useful feature for their community life, by which they can declare that there but for the grace of God go they and somehow survive. Instead they are faced with who they really are themselves and how they are going

94

to live alongside this man who is now clothed and in his right mind. The outcome of this story is two-fold. They ask Jesus to leave. Legion, despite asking if he can follow Jesus, is told to stay.

> 'Go home to your friends and tell them how much the Lord has done for you and how he has had mercy on you.'

Mark 5.19

The legacy of this story is really in the challenge it lays before the Gerasene community, and indeed any human community. What do we do when our perceptions of certain individuals or groups within our communities change? Legion cannot be asked to leave at this point. It would be too easy for the community who have, during his madness, kept him on the edge of expulsion, but for his usefulness in reminding them of what they are not. Self-expulsion would be terribly convenient, for it would mean putting off the questions of why they were now more afraid than before, and how they were going to relate to him differently.

The movement from commitment to community is an essential one for healthy human living. If Christians are to continue to support the principle of public commitment in a culture and social climate that is increasingly disabling itself from such a value, then we have to face the fullest consequences of that principle. Those who join this life of community may not do so in a covert manner, and we should neither expect nor encourage them to do so. Furthermore, it is reasonable to assume that any such community will be affected by the lives of its composite members. Thus the entire community is shaped continually by the dynamics of the individuals within it and the relationships they forge. Those relationships pose a continuous challenge to the entire community and what it understands itself to be. So, if, for example, a marriage breaks down, or an elderly adult in the community dies, or a child is diagnosed as terminally ill, or a baby is born to parents who had been told they were infertile, or the most unlikely person has been caught shoplifting, the entire community is affected by the experience. Individuals within it will process the events and their consequences in different ways. Shock and denial,

95

compassion and solidarity – whatever the response, all are involved because of their commitment to community.

In that sense, then, it is not enough for heterosexual men and women to say, 'I don't mind gays so long as they leave me alone.' It is clear from experience, and from what the Gospels have to say to us about the implicit nature of what it means to live 'in Christ', that this is not an option. There was clear evidence from the couples in this sample that they were neither wanting to be left alone by the rest of the Christian community, nor seeking to live secretly within it. Christians who espouse the value of public commitment need also to accept the reality that a commitment to one individual for life, in public, of necessity means a commitment by that couple to the community they want to be a part of and the rest of the community to them. There is no one part of the body that can say to another, 'I do not need you!'

Notes

1 Stephen Law, *The Xmas Files*, Weidenfeld and Nicolson, 2003, pp. 12ff.
2 Ruth Gledhill, *The Times*, 19 June 2003.
3 Jeffrey Heskins, 'Essentially Reflective' from *The Parish*, ed. Malcolm Torry, Canterbury Press, 2004, pp. 186ff.
4 Andrew Sullivan, *Virtually Normal*, Picador, 1995, p. 133.
5 James Alison, *On Being Liked*, Darton, Longman and Todd, 2003, pp. 65ff.
6 *On Being Liked*, p. 70.
7 *On Being Liked*, p. 72.
8 *On Being Liked*, pp. 71–2.
9 *On Being Liked*, p. 75.
10 James Alison, *Faith Beyond Resentment*, Darton, Longman and Todd, 2001, pp. 126ff.

5

In sickness, health and death

FROM COMMUNITY TO KINGDOM COME

If the injunction to be faithful to death regardless of life's consequences is to stand any chance of realization, in a sense we need
to link the momentum from the commitment of individuals to life
in community into a definitive understanding of what it means to
live within God's Kingdom. An inability to do so would make the
Christian vision of life together no different from any other.

In what is regarded as a latter-day spiritual classic, *Praying the
Kingdom*, Charles Elliott reminds us that according to the Gospels,
when Jesus told his disciples to pray for the Kingdom he seems to
have assumed that they knew how to go about it. His exhortation to
pray that the Kingdom would come was in response to a specific
request. The disciples had not asked what they should pray for, but
how they should pray.[1] There is then a sense in which our appeal for
the Kingdom to come on earth as it is in heaven has something distinctly to do with the way we are with each other and the way we deal
with each other in community.

That in itself must take on the dimension of what Donal Dorr calls
'proclamation by living'.[2] By this I think he means to challenge
Christians to live in community in anticipation of the eschatological
Kingdom – a sort of living the future now. For many Christians the
notion of the Kingdom has an anachronistic feel to it. The Kingdom
of God is something akin to an afterlife reward, depending upon a
mixture of good behaviour and God's grace, and has little to do with
the here and now. But the call to discipleship through Christian community demands that we establish something of the nature of what
we mean by God's Kingdom in the here and now.

In order to determine what that might be, we have to look for symptoms or signs of the Kingdom. That doesn't seem to be so difficult. A careful reading of the Gospels reveals that the seeds of the Kingdom are a set of values that directly contravene the assumptions of many human social cultures, and particularly ones that have been dominated by men. Power and personal advancement are displaced in favour of the otherwise less glamorous values of humility and compassion. The first will be last, we are told, and early Christian communities made bold attempts to pick this up. They seemed to understand, if only for a short while, that to make the Kingdom present, they needed to become communities of transformation. This would entail transforming the way they lived as Christians, with a view to then transforming society as a whole. It would appear that some of the early communities were successful in this. The letter to the Galatians famously declares:

> For as many of you who were baptized into Christ have put on Christ. There is neither Jew nor Greek, there is neither slave nor free, there is neither male nor female; for you are all one in Christ Jesus.

> Galatians 3.26–8

So the desire to inculcate the values of the Kingdom into Christian communities in the here and now requires the need for transformation of individual and corporate consciousness. If the Kingdom is about the way we live alongside one another in those communities then what we have learned from the last chapter is that to expel that which we don't like, or reject that which we simply don't understand or even fear, is probably a failure to utilize these insights.

The tendency within today's Church seems to be either an unwillingness to grasp the nettle of same-sex partnerships, or a failure to know how to go about it. I recently attended a very useful diocesan study day that looked at further issues in human sexuality. What was particularly good, given the hysterical international Church climate, was that it happened at all. Its format was quite formal – a selection of speakers, all ordained, nearly all men, each offering a different point of view, followed by questions from the floor. What was not good was, first, the attitude of many participants, who applauded enthusiastically the speakers whose insights confirmed their own position and resolutely declined to do the same for the speakers whose views they disagreed with, and second, the distinct lack of direction as to where the study day would go next. There was no active encouragement to share the initiative of the day at a grass roots level – New Westminster or Oxford style. It was as though everyone was simply relieved that it was over without any blood on the carpet. Once again those making up the baseline of the Church and its point of view were overlooked.

The most challenging moment of the day was when some of those present shared from the floor how it felt, as gay and lesbian clergy in (often) long-standing partnerships, to be the subject of a study day. A simple but well-made point. The speakers had addressed the already well-rehearsed arguments of same-sex partnerships, but the short comings of an entirely academic presentation were, in a moment, plain for all to see. We were discussing real people living real lives as if they were not there.

Some weeks later, a priest in the diocese circulated an e-mail, to an undisclosed number of recipients, protesting about such open behaviour and describing it as a challenge to the authority of the diocesan bishop. He demanded that all such openness should desist. Whatever prompted him to make this peculiar demand, he had patently failed to see the incongruity of asking his brothers and sisters in the Body of Christ to be invisible or go away because he was not ready for them.

There has long been a trend in gay circles to live inside a sub-culture that is affirming of gay men and lesbian women as people while protesting at a climate of indifference and intolerance within wider society. The proliferation of gay-friendly pubs and clubs is a mark of this and something that can be found in most urban centres. The sample of clergy in this study were all aware of that culture, and some had participated in it. But nearly all were looking for something different. It wasn't that there was no value in that culture, it simply didn't cater for them and their needs.

I think that both of us have taken the choice that we would rather live in a wider community than just in the gay community. I know that there are some people who live just in the gay community because that is where it is safest, and maybe it is safer there. I think it is very easy to escape into a completely gay lifestyle and ignore a lot of the reality of life.

Male priest with partner 31 years

It's odd about the gay community because we find when we are drawing up a list for a party or whatever, we don't actually circulate in a gay community any more. That's probably more to do with our age.

Male priest with partner 28 years

I have never been sure how this sub-culture ever came about, whether it was at the behest of gay men and lesbian women who simply preferred each other's company or whether it was a sign of or protest about their growing sense of alienation or unacceptability in a wider community. Certainly such a sub-culture has similar identifying features with foreign (usually Jewish) cultures that formed the ghettos of European cities. They were initially places of identity and security for those living in them. Families knew each other and everyone could look out for one another. Customs and other ways of being were accepted and didn't have to be explained. For those living outside these communities, and the authorities which governed them, it was a way of creating cultural boundaries and of maintaining control. At one level, everyone gained by this way of living.

From ghetto to Egypt

The term ghetto now tends to mean something quite negative. It is a place to fear if you do not belong to it. The word comes from the Italian word meaning 'foundry', and relates to a medieval foundry in Venice, which later became the site that the Jewish community inhabited. However, it has its deeper roots in the Latin *Aegyptus*, meaning Egypt, with, presumably allusions to the Jews held in captivity under Pharaoh. We often speak of a 'ghetto mentality' as relating

8

to a place where groups isolate themselves as if those in them are entirely responsible for their existence. What this masks is the collusion that the ghetto mentality fosters. The ghetto exists in many different shapes and forms, but they all have the same purpose. On the one hand, they offer identifiable safety, at one level, to those in them, and on the other they constitute a convenient screen for those who cannot or will not relate to them. However, there comes a time when those inside decide that the ghetto is no longer a satisfactory place to be. It becomes a place, like Egypt for the Jewish slaves, of oppression and repression. They want to leave; Pharaoh doesn't want them to. They want to be free; Pharaoh wants to control them. They want to take their place in the wider world; Pharaoh fears cultural contamination from them.

To emerge from the ghetto is a fearful thing. Not everyone wants to leave it – 'we would have been better off in Egypt' – and those that do are often treated as a spreading virus: 'acceptance of same-sex couples will undermine marriage and the security of children . . .'

> *I hope that one day the idea of a gay community will become a thing of the past. Society is mixed and I am looking to integrate, not segregate, though I do recognize that as a temporary measure we need to organize ourselves to be an effective presence that will, hopefully, bring about integration.*
>
> *Male ordinand with partner 7 years*

There is ample evidence that many Christians, and certainly most of the clergy in this sample, while they are glad of the support found in the sub-culture they called the gay community, preferred to be a part of a wider culture. The problem about moving on from the sub-culture (in the case of those who had at any time been a part of it) was the fear of rejection in wanting to take an open place within the wider culture of the Church.

Living the ethic of gratuity

When the Israelites finally left Egypt their liberation began, and as we read on we see that while in the desert place, coming to terms with who they were and exactly what they had done, and in the giving of the Law, their sense of liberation became complete. It is hard to imagine how the giving of the Law could be liberating, because we tend to regard the rule of law and the enforcement of law as a system of 'do nots'. The law of the land is something that tells us what we may not do. The gift of the Law to the people of Israel was far more positive than that. It was a gift that defined the Covenant relationship between God and Israel and was seen as a reflection of God's loving generosity towards the nation. Further on in his book, Charles Elliott says that for the Israelite, at its best the Law was working out what loving-kindness meant in everyday relationships. As God had liberated Israel from the ghetto of Egyptian slavery, so they were to celebrate that liberation, not with self-indulgence, but by showing the same loving generosity to all others and particularly those who had no rights or any particular claim on that generosity.

> It is this ethic that we need to let come alive in us. It is the ethic that I shall call, after Jean Vanier, the ethic of gratuity. That is a word that many people find difficult. 'To people in my station in life,' said a wealthy but well meaning friend, 'gratuity is what you give the boot boy.' Perhaps, but in its original, deeper meaning gratuity was the virtue of overwhelming love expressing itself in almost excessive generosity.[3]

What is clear is that inclusion in the ghetto or within a sub-culture is not the same as inclusion within the community. Whatever its merits, the sub-culture remains what it is – a sub-culture. The liberating movement into a wider community demands a response from the participants in that community, and if the Law is liberating as we see it lived out in the person of Jesus Christ, then that response has to be a reflection of his life. We need to experience a paradigm shift, what Elliott calls from 'egocentricity to gratuity'. This means a translation from intellectual status to practical reality of what it means to live the gratuitous love that is God's Kingdom.

> For the natural human pressures are to cut oneself off from the full grandeur of God's love and seek to contain it, control it, tame it,

make it predictable and manageable. Most people are deeply frightened of the unconditional love and its power to expand the freedom of the loved one. They therefore want to institutionalize it, regulate it, surround it with restrictions, conventions – anything to keep it safe.[4]

None of the participants accused the Church as an institution of being particularly unloving as they reflected upon their life within it, but for nearly everyone the frailty of the Church was marked by its apparent inability to love unconditionally as challenged by the law of gratuitous loving. A particular irony was that the couples almost without exception found a greater degree of acceptance and affirmation for who they were as gay men and lesbian women, and what they did as priests, from people who were not part of the Church, or who had left the Church because of this perception.

I do get a sense that some of our secular gay friends who aren't Christians do find it easier because we are together. People have an impression of the Church as judgemental.

Male priest with partner 5 years

We have a lot of friends, quite a few of whom are gay, and a lot of those people have dismissed the Church as being oppressive. They find it interesting how we manage to support an organization that doesn't seem to support us.

Male ordinand with partner 7 years

I used to be part of a group of lesbian women who met regularly to socialize, and I think that initially coming out to them as a priest was almost harder than the other way round. I as a priest have been part of a structure that has been extremely oppressive in the way that it has treated gay and lesbian people. In a sense the Church is at the root of some of the nasty homophobic killings that we have seen in the USA.

Female priest with partner 6 years

*Many of our friends who aren't part of a church can't understand why we stay,
but at least they know that if they want to talk they can. In our context we are
a model of a stable, loving relationship – something that they think the
Church ought to be glad to promote.*

Male priest with partner 20 years

And there were instances when because of this dynamic some found
an enhanced ministry to those outside the Church.

*There are at least six gay establishments in my parish and I think that it is
quite important to go there if I can. Recently I heard the saddest story, when I
bumped into someone from one of these places who told me that they had
recently had a bereavement and couldn't find a sympathetic priest to do a wake
with them because they were gay. I would have been glad to have helped them
and told them so. I plan to visit there regularly now.*

Female priest with partner 3 years

*There are some gay people who face me with questions of how I can be gay and
a Christian in a Church that seems to be saying hostile things to lesbian and
gay people. But many of them realize that the Church is a much more complex
place and that it is difficult to live within it with integrity and then they realize
that it happens to gay people in the secular world too. They encounter situations there where they too are compromised. I find that this often opens doors
for me in my ministry to help them find a way of interpreting what is happening to them.*

Male priest with partner 6 years

Three priests found that although they were not seeking a specialist
gay ministry, there were couples and individuals who searched them
out particularly because they felt able to identify with them and trust
them.

*Word does go round the grapevine either that I am a gay priest or that I am
gay friendly. For example I took a funeral of a gay person recently, someone*

who was quite prominent on the gay scene. As an evangelical I used to find that other evangelicals who were discovering that they were gay, who didn't easily relate to groups like LGCM, needed someone with whom they could talk the theological language of the evangelical community.

Male priest with partner 15 years

Recently Patsy and Rose asked me to bless the house they had just moved into. One of them is a Christian though she doesn't come to church here. They needed someone who would understand their situation and it was a real privilege to do it.

Female priest with partner 2 years

There have been three or four people who have been specifically referred to me because I am in a partnership. They come specifically to talk to me about matters concerning sexuality. So, being a priest and being gay has really helped in situations like that.

Male priest with partner 20 years

Most found that being in a partnership was helpful at times when engaging in pastoral work. There were occasions when the isolation of being gay or lesbian within the Church brought a degree of affinity in some pastoral relationships. Likewise, those who felt themselves the direct object of the Church's judgement approached them for counsel and discovered common ground and a sense of safety in the pastoral encounter.

Some of the pain I have experienced as one on the edge of the Church since I was a teenager has helped me be compassionate. Sometimes that being on the edge is comfortable because you are so different, but it is also a difficult place to be because there isn't an opportunity to be 'in' because you don't fit and many of the people that I listen to have just that experience. They don't fit in or belong.

Female ordinand with partner 1 year

Being a minority within a majority community and having to come through some personal struggle and some personal discovery of who you are, rather than walking into boxes that are there for you makes for some sense of common ground on which to relate to other people. Having been through it I find it a useful gift to have as a priest.

Male priest with partner 15 years

The couples that I met were all, without exception, very open about themselves and their relationships. Their inclination to openness made it all the harder for them to compromise who they naturally were for the sake of ecclesial protocol and those clergy and laity who seemed to resent their existence.

The biggest hindrance I have is the need to be hidden from some people. I like to think that I am quite an integrated person and so to have to keep splitting myself to oblige the Church or lesbian company is not something I want to do and I think it could be such a good example.

Female priest with partner 14 years

For all of them, the experience of having a partner with whom they could share the burdens of ministry and life was both life enhancing and fulfilling. It made all the difference.

Being in partnership with him has made a difference. I take more time out than I did. Certainly I am more settled and have more confidence.

He has always been constant. The very thing that drew me to him was his honesty from the first time we met. He doesn't always see things but he has always been constant.

Male priest and partner together 2 years

The search for gratuitous love, the unconditional love of God, begins within our capacity for human love. Thus it is a love that is transforming in its power. The signs of that love are the radical signs of

God's Kingdom or Reign, and they are to be sought, and found (if we are consistent with the Gospels), in the lives of the misunderstood, the despised and the rejected (in Gospel terms, the poor). What makes it a transforming love is not simply that God loves the poor as a result, or even that they come to realize that God loves them. Instead the 'poor' become the vehicle of God's love to enable others to be transformed by it. That lies at the core of what it means to be Christian. The challenge for the whole Church is that here, within it, are these faithful and stable models of relationship – examples from the leaders of Christ's Church to those they minister to. Is it possible that they might be seen as signs of God's gratuitous love?

> *Being a Christian informs my life in a way that I don't find restrictive. On the contrary, I find it liberating and I find my partnership something that I want to celebrate and bring with me. It is not that I am living my life according to a heterosexual pattern as some might think, but one that is born out of the love ethic. So, if you talk about the requirement of, say, fidelity, it is not so much a requirement as something that grows out of one's love. I don't want to live in any other way.*
>
> Male ordinand with partner 7 years

The Kingdom as crisis

In the synoptic traditions, the challenge of the Kingdom proves too much for the established religious authorities of the day. With a few notable exceptions, the message of the Kingdom as preached and lived out by Jesus is rejected. The established leadership of synagogue and temple are depicted as collectively adopting the logic of Caiaphas; namely, it is expedient to sacrifice the innocent for the sake of the institution. That tends to be how institutional authority reacts when faced with radical changes that have captured the popular imagination. The Church has experienced this time and again, most recently over the ordination of women to the historic priesthood. For years some saw this as an issue that would divide the Church, driving it towards irreparable schism. As the debate rolled on, those opposed to it ran out of persuasive arguments and instead turned up the volume on unity. For years those women who felt called by God to be priests and deacons waited, yet their call to priesthood was the expedient sacrifice for institutional unity. Mercifully, this situation did not ultimately prevail; ironically the logic of Caiaphas was exposed for what it is – a fallacy. The ordination of women in the Church did what these issues do, namely reveal the differences of individuals and the wealth of collective diversity in the Church, and throw down the gauntlet to the Church to grow up and learn to handle it. It is precisely where we now stand on the inclusion of gay men and women in the Church and particularly those clergy in open, faithful partnerships. If this is what it means to be a Church in crisis then it is no bad thing, and key to understanding the Kingdom as we hear it proclaimed in the Gospels.

> The disciples of John came to him and said, 'John the Baptist has sent us to you saying, "Are you the one who is to come or shall we look for another?"' In that hour he cured many of diseases and plagues and evil spirits, and on many that were blind he bestowed sight. And he answered them, 'Go and tell John what you have seen and heard: the blind receive their sight, the lame walk, lepers are cleansed and the deaf hear, the dead are raised up and the poor have good news preached to them. And blessed are those who take no offence at me.'
>
> Luke 7.20–3

In this passage from Luke's Gospel we have a manifesto précis of the Kingdom. Jesus is portrayed, in conversation with the disciples of John, as one who describes the essentials of the Kingdom by its signs and symptoms. This must have been infuriating for John's disciples because it doesn't directly answer their question. They want to know if Jesus is the one they have been on the lookout for. He tells them to relay the signs that they see. What they have to do is assess the situation and come to a decision based on an act of faith. If the signs speak of the Kingdom that they have been waiting and praying for, then what does it say of the identity of the bearer? The decision is theirs.

This is a common pattern in most of the healing miracles described in the synoptic Gospels. In proclaiming the Kingdom, the healing miracles (more usefully described as 'signs' in the fourth Gospel), take up about one-fifth of the Gospel material that we have. Clearly they are significant, but in a contemporary culture such as our own in Western Europe and North America, we have foolishly bought into an individualistic mind-set that directs our thinking towards the individual recipient of the healing. Look at what it has done for this man, or that woman, we tell ourselves, without ever considering whether it is doing anything for us.

The healing work of Jesus is never really described as a private thing between God and one individual. It is not simply a test of faith for the sick person, who receives the reward of their regained health, having passed with flying colours. It is a public, effective sign, something done in front of witnesses. But those who witness are not passive, as though in an audience watching a play; they are active participants who are brought to the point of crisis. I don't mean 'crisis' in its everyday sense of a temporary, if acute, problem, but as a biblical technical term. Crisis means judgement and it is part of the vocabulary of the Last Days. When Jesus heals someone, it is not simply a crisis for the one who receives the healing; it is a crisis for all those who witness it. Like the disciples of John, they have to come to a decision. The healing has implications for them too. It is a Kingdom moment in which faith is inspired and the Kingdom entered into by way of understanding; or it is rejected, leading to connivance and scheming to silence the perpetrator, or simply not understood.

The lack of understanding is most cleverly depicted in the Gospel of Mark. Here, the identity of Jesus as the Kingdom personified is only gradually grasped. In chapter 1, Jesus heals a man in the synagogue of an unclean spirit. The response of the witnesses is surprise – 'What is this? A new teaching?' In chapter 2 he heals the paralytic let down through the roof by his friends and makes a provocative statement about forgiving sins. The crowd responds by saying, 'We never saw anything like this!' By chapter 3 he has healed a man with a withered arm on the Sabbath, and the religious authorities respond with a plot to destroy him. In chapter 4 he stills the storm which prompts his own followers to ask, 'Who is this?' By chapter 8 he has fed 5,000 people, walked on water and fed a further 4,000. Only then, when he asks them outright who they think he is, does Peter declare him to be the Messiah, although he fails to see that this Kingdom is one that is based on gratuitous love not on military might. So it continues to chapter 15, when the final sign of this love, the crucifixion itself, inspires the centurion to the declaration of faith in Jesus as the Son of God. Only then is it made clear that Jesus is as Jesus does.

Gratuitous love as pastoral care

Being in the Kingdom then has something to do with recognition and choice. What we often don't realize is just how astonishing and radical were the promises and claims of this Kingdom vision. The society into which Jesus introduces the vision is clearly defined in terms of its social order. The humble and meek would never expect to be preferred by God in place of the rich and famous. To tell someone that they will see God is practically a blasphemy and to encourage the poor to imagine that the Kingdom is theirs is either lunacy or an incitement to rebellion. But if we look at, for example, Matthew's beatitudes, we have a summary manifesto of the Kingdom. We see that God's concern with creation and the desire for a covenant relationship with human beings is rich and transforming. This is not because anyone can claim this relationship by right or social status, class or wealth, but because it is offered to those who have no claim upon it. What makes our response to the Kingdom crisis so critical and even frightening is that it dares us to believe in the almost unbelievable. We are to look for God's gratuitous love and the Kingdom signs in those places we have hitherto written off as impossible for God to live and work through. I would suggest that we extend that search to the relationships of these gay and lesbian couples.

To this day Alistair Campbell's *Rediscovering Pastoral Care*[5] remains one of my favourite pastoral theology books. It was first published in the year I was ordained, but it has continued to be an inspiring book for me. I remember wondering, having just staggered through three years of academic theology and a year of practical training, how on earth would I connect everything that I had learned in theory with what lay ahead of me in the field of pastoral practice? Campbell succeeded in proving for me that theological thought does not have to be obtuse, nor theological ideas remote if they can be communicated in language that draws on everyday images. He does this by reflecting on old images of pastoral care and through them discovering new and exciting insights that describe God in action. For me, the search for appropriate images or models of God in the face of human experience and relationships has been a constant challenge, and one that presents itself to us now as the issues of sexual orientation and sexual expression rumble on in the Church. The search for pastoral images of God in the relationships of gay and lesbian couples has to remain a serious part of that challenge, although we might be required to offer a critical review of the images discovered. Why? Because images have a habit of becoming dated and what was conveyed by an image in one generation might be completely lost on another.

Campbell constantly reminds me of this when I want to talk about 'pastoral care'. It is, of course, a phrase derived from the idea of shepherding. This powerful image of hardiness and physical courage, however, developed into the rather effete and sentimental figure of the Good Shepherd. Worse still, the shepherd has come to be depicted as paternalistic, knowing best, while the sheep are errant and feckless. Translated into the contemporary Church context these are not helpful interpretations of what was once a radical image. What Campbell seeks to do, and perhaps what we need to do, as faith communities reflecting on what gay and lesbian partnerships might have to offer as models of pastoral care, is to see if there is anything worth recovering in the images that are brought to light.

What is it like, being a priest and having my primary human relationship with another woman? It's living an impossibility, it's listening to people on the radio or in conversation talking about 'them' and knowing it's me. It's living with a 'white noise' of anxiety and fear that is a tinnitus I can't shake. This fear is debilitating and echoes around the institution I move in. I can see it in the eyes of others too; the fear of being 'found' or the fear of being 'wrong' or the fear of having to make a relationship with someone they don't understand.[6]

When I read this extract from the discussion document produced by the House of Bishops' Group on *Issues in Human Sexuality*, I am struck by its agony. The fear and paralysis it induces in the anonymous voice is quite harrowing. What this priest describes is a sense of being a non-person. She serves an institution in which she runs the risk of exposure and condemnation as if she were engaged in criminal activity. That fear of the judgemental Church envelops her; she sees it in others like her, and the temptation is to find a man to deflect suspicion and keep up appearances.

The vulnerability of being ordained and gay is evident in the lives of any who have either tried to live openly or who have been 'outed' by others. The need for support in order simply to sustain the most rudimentary elements of life is important. But where does this help come from?

For some of those I interviewed there was support within the Church structures they inhabited. This existed at different levels, but it was inconsistent across the country. Others found support in the acceptance of being known within a congregation, but this too had degrees of inconsistency. For some the fear of discovery was very real. But for most, the principal source of support and encouragement was the partnership they had and because of that they felt themselves to be more effective ministers and priests.

Gratuitous love as pastoral care revealed itself first in the support the couples were able to offer each other by listening. It became emphatically ironic that the one major request these gay and lesbian couples made from the Church was the very image they modelled for each other. The kind of listening that Bonhoeffer described in Chapter 2 and which the Lambeth Conference bishops had called for was central to nearly every couple who spoke to me. That listening was critical in three particular areas: patient listening to the events of daily life, the listening to encourage one another, and the listening that allowed them to challenge one another.

I think that we do a fair amount of listening to each other. There is the daily stuff of working through the day. There is the cheering each other up, as it were. I think there are the testing things out kind of thing with each other. So if he has to give a talk for his teaching programme then he will try out those ideas on me. At home, sermons are usually heard before they are broadcast. Things like that.

Male priest with partner 15 years

For those who were unable to live with each other all of the time this listening had to be done at distance and required commitment.

Talking on the phone we share what is going on in our lives and so we talk on the phone every day. He takes an interest in everything that goes on here and because he knows a lot he is a good sounding board.

Male priest with partner 2 years

This kind of listening sometimes had a sacrificial nature to it.

He listens, and I mean that in every sense; it is a good quality of listening. He is extremely patient with the demands of a parish and my own perfectionism, wanting to get the parish right and give people that sense that they are being listened to, which will often diminish our own quality of family life, and he lives with that!

Male priest with partner 5 years

Second, gratuitous love as pastoral care revealed itself in the model of service and servant. This was particularly apparent in times of crisis or illness or bereavement.

I supported her through the menopause and I haven't had the best of health myself, having been into hospital over the last few years. It is not easy and made no easier by having Church people around and she having to be invisible in the background. There was a time earlier this year when I was really ill and she felt like she was just the person coming along with the clean pyjamas.

Yes. I felt a bit like a girl Friday or the handywoman and I know that I am not the best nurse in the world.

Female priest and partner 13 years

The model of servant, rather like that of shepherd, is one that often fails to communicate its authentic nature. The servant has shades of social inferiority or even dependency, which is, of course, not that offered by Jesus of the Gospels. The servanthood of Christ is one that he voluntarily enters into because it is a constituent component of the Kingdom he is describing. To serve as Christ serves becomes a metaphor of mutuality. Couples spoke of their serving support for each other leading them towards a partnership of equals. If there was any dependency, it was a mutual one.

Before ordination I was wrongly diagnosed with an incurable and debilitating illness. There were doubts as to whether the Church would ordain me and it was an awful period for me. Because it was early on in our relationship, I told him that I didn't expect him to take me on as a cripple or whatever I was going to become, but he was supportive and in the end we pulled through together. I couldn't have done it without him.

Male priest with partner 8 years

At the time my father developed Alzheimer's and through the subsequent bereavement I don't know what I would have done without him. It made us realize our own mortality and that the time will come when it will be just us two. What do we do? We have to learn to reach out more. He has been an enormous strength to me and I know that he would say the same of me.

Male priest with partner 20 years

The expression of mutuality as a quality of servanthood is the catalyst for confronting and enabling others to look again at these lives in partnership and see them in a new way. One couple described how a crisis and the example of his partner transformed the thinking and attitude of his hesitant family in rural Cornwall.

Some years ago I was diagnosed with a cancer that required an operation and radiotherapy. He was marvellous and became my prime carer. The whole experience helped me see that there was more to life than work. Our relationship and time together became more important after that. But in addition my family came to see things differently. They had found my sexuality and our relationship very difficult, but they saw something very practical in action at that point. They saw him in a different light; no longer as some kind of monster who turned me gay, but as one who was a very supportive and loving part of my life.

Male priest with partner 15 years

Finally, gratuitous love as pastoral care revealed itself as solidarity in community. While most of those taking part had already indicated that what is deemed the gay 'scene' was either no longer part of their world or never had been, they found value in the creation of wider support systems where they could be openly themselves without fear of reprisal or recrimination. Chief among these was the creation of the Clergy Consultation, a support network for gay and lesbian clergy and ordinands with guaranteed confidentiality. The Consultation meets regularly and involves hundreds of clergy throughout the country. Membership is by invitation only. While many were grateful for pressure groups like LGCM (the Lesbian and Gay Christian Movement) and Changing Attitudes, some found that the kind of political activism such groups engaged in, though valuable, was not the arena they could most comfortably engage in.

I am involved with the Clergy Consultation and have some involvement with the Human Sexuality Joint Strategy Group, which includes members of LGCM and Changing Attitudes and General Synod. These groups try to share ideas and work together and that is not always easy. The problem with these pressure groups is that they do not always represent the view that I feel comfortable with. I know there are times when it is good to have political pressure in place, but I am quite gentle by nature and I think that quite simply by being who you are you begin to exert an acceptable level of pressure for change.

Female priest with partner 3 years

I am a member of LGCM, but it is a bit like my membership of the Labour Party. I feel it is important to do it but I haven't been actively involved. Groups like that are important because campaign is necessary alongside other means of change. Sometimes the voices are a bit shrill and if it were me I would be doing it differently, but I am glad they exist.

Male priest with partner 15 years

I joined LGCM for a year but didn't renew my membership. I joined Changing Attitudes after that and then found out about the Clergy Consultation in the last year and went along to that. That is the group I have found the most supportive. So we travel up to London for the Consultation meeting and that has been great because we have been able to meet people face to face, which has been invaluable. Some of the people you meet you just wouldn't have any idea about in the ordinary course of things, and because the Consultation is a confidential group and you have to be introduced to it, there is a greater feeling of safety in it.

Female ordinand with partner 12 years

Everyone welcomed the sense of support and solidarity, but particularly the women, although lesbian clergy and ordinands opting to join these organizations often found themselves a minority group within a minority group! That being so, it was difficult for them to influence the way the group was run or to identify with and feel represented by the views of some of the more outspoken gay men.

The difficulty for me is that the spokespersons for those groups are sometimes people to whom I can't really relate. It tends to be the male voices that are heard and the types of voice are not those of moderation, and for me that doesn't sit with trying to live a Christ-like life, trying to be faithful to one's vocation as a priest.

Female priest with partner 3 years

Nearly everyone described a feeling of support from their local church community. There were few exceptions. Most described a learning curve in relating to members of their local church. How would the

membership respond to their partners? Would the 'traditional' clergy
wife or husband provide the pattern to follow?

> *My local church has been all right and they recognized that he is part of the
> scenario when I was sick. Sometimes we are struggling to find appropriate
> ways because he is not the vicar's wife or husband, but he is something else and
> we haven't got the right language for it. What do you do for him in this situ-
> ation? Do you buy a bunch of flowers or send a card?*
>
> Male priest with partner 15 years

In town or country, it was often the least likely members of the congregation who were the most supportive.

> *Like the Barringtons, a pair of funny old trouts in church, a straight couple
> and as conventional and establishment as you could wish to meet, but very
> supportive and would never dream of inviting one of us without the other.*
>
> Male priest with partner 32 years

In the wider local community, there were also signs of support and
acceptance from unexpected sources.

> *There is a 78-year-old man next door, not the place you would expect imme-
> diate acceptance, and not long after we had moved in we bumped into him on
> the pavement outside and he said, 'You must come and see us. Just pop in one
> evening and say hello. You know, if you have had a row and one of you wants
> to get out of the house, just come and sit with us and watch television if you
> want for an hour or two.' He just treats us as if we are normal.*
>
> Male partner of priest 5 years

One or two had media experience and noted that in the national
climate, the whole gay issue had changed noticeably in the last 30
years.

> *Elderly ladies will send cards saying they thought the letter in The Times was
> absolutely appalling. E-mail from people you hadn't heard from in years*

saying the same. What you don't get any more are the sacks of hate mail. In recent months I have done BBC 4, the Telegraph, the Guardian and other bits. He has done Radio 2 and we do some media together. The great joke is that officially I am the only gay priest in the Church of England. Several years ago we did some media thing, and of course gay only happens in London and here we were, middle class, middle aged and boring and living way beyond Essex.

Male priest with partner 20 years

If gratuitous love expresses itself as pastoral care, then the signs of the Kingdom go on throwing up surprises. While confusion continues in some levels of the Church with regard to its gay and lesbian clergy, the laity at grass roots appears to be tackling it and simply getting on with it. Whatever else is happening, there is some progress as the experience of meeting gay and lesbian couples confronts us with our prejudices. We are faced with that moment of 'crisis' in which we have to make a judgement, and then continue the journey. One participant described it as such and found that it resonated with some of the great sacred texts of scripture. As we continue to grow in understanding, there is always a sense in which we are 'guests in each other's environments', as he put it. Inviting each other into this environment and allowing the experience of participation is the key to growth and change, new perspective and fuller understanding. It was ever thus.

We always seem to be guests in each other's environments, sojourning in a strange land. People forget that this is how Moses describes himself and it is key to the experience of being human. At the end of Deuteronomy Moses dies and the children of Israel are still in the desert. This is a key narrative about people leaving slavery, grappling with freedom in the desert place and how in the desert they have to find ways of living together responsibly and lovingly. At the end of the story they haven't got to where they are going but they are on their way there. To some degree in the relationship I have, I identify with that, not in the sense of place, but in terms of life itself. It is here, I think that we do, all of us, grapple with the nature of freedom, and within freedom it is about making the choices to create community, fellowship and relationship with others. That is what they do in the desert and that is what we do as people.

Male priest with partner 2 years

Listening, service and the solidarity of community are three pastoral images that emerge from these relationships and define for the participants what it means for each of them to live faithfully together under God. The call to holy living is not shirked in these relationships, and this is addressed in greater depth in the next chapter. However, pastoral images are not merely pointers to holy living, but also a means by which God is identified in us and to us, and this should not be bypassed here. The images of God as one who listens, as one who serves and one who stands among us are well-established, in both scripture and the traditions of the Church. That these images are also found in the testimonies of these couples attests further to their authenticity and in so doing challenges us to rethink our current standing on gay and lesbian relationships within the Church, both clergy and laity. Should the whole Church meet that challenge, it could mean a very different future for an entire section of the world-wide Church community, currently alienated in many quarters, vilified by some, ignored by others and often misunderstood. Many hoped the Church would meet that challenge and looked forward to a better future in the Church together.

I hope for a Church that will have the courage to be prophetic on this issue and for its leaders who are privately supportive of people like me to say so openly. I would like the Church to move to a point where our relationship could be blessed and recognized and, yes, so that we could grow old together until we die.

And also for it to recognize that being in relationship actually makes us stronger people, better able to give more to those we minister to and more enriched as people by not having to live in lonely isolation.

Female priests together 3 years

What we hope for is a willingness on the part of the bishops of the Anglican Communion to acknowledge not only that there are gay and lesbian priests doing a wonderful service in their dioceses, but that if those same priests, with their partners are honest enough to be open about those partnerships, from which they live and derive support and comfort and energy to sustain their

119

ministries, that they should not then be punished or penalized for their ministry in the Church.

Female ordinand with partner 1 year

I hope that the Church becomes a bit more real. Experiencing people exercising that gift of love, inclusiveness and acceptance, I realize that if it is not of God then the Church's God is less than the people I encounter. I don't believe that.

Male priest with partner 2 years

I hope for complete integration and acceptance and I hope that we will grow old together loving God and each other.

Male ordinand with partner 6 years

I hope that both he and I will continue as a partnership for life and that the future will allow me to exercise a ministry more freely than is currently possible.

Male priest with partner 15 years

The things that we talk about are a future. When she retires we hope for a more public shared ministry because we know that we are a good team and to be able to live that out more fully would be great; for example we had someone come and talk to the parish about youth work and youth ministry and it was the classic thing of what you need is a nice couple who will invite these youngsters in and make them feel at home. And I thought, 'We could do that!' We have got those skills and gifts and I know it could work as well as if we were any married couple.

Female priest with partner 2 years

Notes

1   Charles Elliott, *Praying the Kingdom*, Darton, Longman and Todd, 1985, p. 22.
2   Donal Dorr, *Spirituality and Justice*, Gill and Macmillan, 1989, p. 100.

3 *Praying the Kingdom*, p. 61.
4 *Praying the Kingdom*, p. 64.
5 Alistair V. Campbell, *Rediscovering Pastoral Care*, Darton, Longman and Todd, 1981.
6 House of Bishops' Group, *Some Issues in Human Sexuality: A Guide to the Debate*, Church House Publishing, 2003, p. 251.

6

According to God's Holy Law

FAITHFUL, INTIMATE AND HOLY LIVING

The Holy One is the One whom one can never search for in vain.[1]

If living in the Kingdom leads us into an understanding of God's law as a gift of gratuitous love, then the challenge of living it out ultimately helps us define our relationship with God. The way we live it out gives expression to the gift. But we need to remember this is God's *holy* law and it is only realized in the lives that fall under the influence of what it means to live as God's gratuitous love. Thus, because it is God's gift and not simply a human achievement, it lies at the heart of the call to holy living. But what exactly does that mean? What does it mean to be called to holiness? In the marriage service opposite-sex couples pledge themselves to each other, 'for better or worse, richer or poorer, in sickness and health until death – according to God's holy law'. Given the absence of any authorized liturgies for the blessing of same-sex couples in their unions, how do they see their relationships reflecting the call to holiness? What does it mean to live a holy life?

Like much religious language, the language of holiness is an endangered species. Outside of the Church most people feel uncomfortable with it or simply don't know what it means. I recently attended a conference on ethical investment at which one of the speakers began his paper by declaring that he was dropping the term 'ethical' and replacing it with 'beneficial'. The word 'ethical' was clearly so loaded with what he perceived as religious baggage that he dispensed with it and substituted another. In doing so, he altered the direction of the conference. He failed to address his own conspicuous inability to see the difference, or his disinclination to try. I am not suggesting that ethical language and holy language are the same, but they do seem to occupy the same cell on death row in a secular context that finds them either meaningless or a challenge that simply draws a blank.

What it meant to live a holy life was the most challenging part of the reflective process for many of the couples interviewed for this book. Some, like the young man at the conference on ethical investment, simply described it in a language that did have some meaning for them.

> I wouldn't choose those words holy living, or holy law, but I suppose it is important to be moral and good, honest and trustful and sometimes take high moral ground.
>
> Partner to female priest together 14 years

> I think it is about goodness in a sense of loving thy neighbour, treating others in a way that you would like to be treated yourself.
>
> Partner to male priest together 5 years

Others saw it in terms of a personal lifestyle.

> For me I think it is expressed in a simplicity of lifestyle and giving priority to human relationships.
>
> Male priest with partner 6 years

Still others saw it as raising God to consciousness in everyday living, describing it as something akin to Brother Lawrence's Practice of the Presence of God.

> For me it would be being aware of the presence of God and trying to live out the example, not necessarily in the practical terms but in the essence of his being; encouraging people to have a full life and be themselves the best way possible.
>
> Male priest with partner 32 years

Others saw it in practical social terms.

> For me the commandment is very simple. It is about Good News for the poor, freedom for those in captivity and bringing sight to the blind. That is the

meeting of the two testaments. It is what I am about and I think that is what holiness was for Jesus and should be for us.

Female priest with partner 5 years

Everyone struggled to come to a definitive statement, but wrestled positively with what they thought they meant by the call to holy living. The 12 bishops and primates who met in the aftermath of the 1998 Lambeth Conference had also struggled, and reported that they had 'not been able to reach a common mind regarding a single pattern for holy living for homosexual people'. To the cynical in the aftermath of Lambeth 1998 this could be seen as the easy way out taken by a group of men fearing to disagree with each other, but I think that would be unfair. This is borne out in our research findings: what became obvious was that no single pattern for holy living could effectively be prescribed for all. What the couples came to see of God was brought to consciousness through the unique circumstances of their given situation and how they tried to interpret that situation through sacred texts, the insights of tradition and how they reasoned in the light of experience. In any event, should any of us really be hoping for prescriptive pronouncements from 'above' on holiness and holy living that apply to all in every circumstance and context? Does this not remove the responsibility for discovering what holy living means to each individual?

If whatever we mean by holiness is seen to emerge from this notion of the Kingdom we have been exploring through its sacred envoy 'gratuitous love', then we already know that defining holiness in the abstract will be difficult, if not impossible. Living within the Kingdom takes holy living beyond the safety of theoretical speculation and into the realm of engagement by participation.

There is no getting around this. Active participation in the search for the mystery of God engages us and this involves risk. Donald Nicholl in his book *Holiness* tells the story of the brilliant German thinker Max Scheler, who converted to Catholicism at the age of 42 and became an ardent expounder of sanctity. But while he was able to wax eloquently in his lectures about the great mystics, what he spoke about became increasingly distanced from who he was. When the Archbishop of Cologne challenged him on this he told the prelate that he only pointed the way; a sign did not have to go where it points. What he failed to see was that in the practice of holy living this is not an option. In the end we have to go in the direction we point or decline into the kind of loneliness that Scheler's life eventually became.[2]

The writer of Genesis records the story of Jacob on the eve of meeting his brother Esau for the first time since tricking him out of his birthright. Whether or not it is a metaphor in which he wrestles with his conscience or with God, the writer tells us that it is only after Jacob (whose name means the one who ousts another by underhand methods) wrestles with the unnamed man at Peniel (meaning I have seen God) that he is named Israel (the one who perseveres with God). We cannot expect to commit ourselves to holy living, and learn from the insights of others, without the risk of being changed.

Who or what is holy?

Holiness is often defined as a state in which persons or things are set apart for the purposes of being consecrated to God. In the Judaic-Christian scriptures there are three detectable strands within the biblical tradition that describe an understanding of holiness. They are distinct but not necessarily unrelated to each other.

The first is sometimes called the *priestly* perspective. This emphasizes God's 'otherness'. In other words, when we try to talk about God we have to begin with what we know. What we know is the experience of being human. God is not a human being and so the things that we associate with being human, like behaviour, values and attitude, are not necessarily the things that define God. So God is separate in the sense that God is not to be identified with creation *per se*. 'My ways are not your ways,' is a frequently heard acclaim in the Judaic scriptures and Moses is accorded as saying of God, 'Who is like you, magnificent in holiness?' (Exodus 15.11).

The second is the *prophetic* understanding. What this does is describe a relationship between worship, the call to social justice and the often recorded need for God's people to mend their ways or change their hearts. We find examples of this in passages like the call of Isaiah (Isaiah 6.3), which takes place in the context of worship and prayer, an important scripture that is replicated in the book of Revelation. In the mystical Gospel of John, Jesus prays to God as 'Holy Father' (John 17.11). The synoptic Gospels all describe Jesus as 'the Holy One of God' (Mark 1.24). Exorcised unclean spirits are usually the ones to do this! Jesus is never attributed as describing *himself* as holy. Matthew and Luke both describe Jesus teaching his disciples to 'hallow the name of God' (Matthew 6.9; Luke 11.2).

The third is sometimes called a *wisdom* understanding of holiness. What this means is that while this particular perspective of holiness is still distinctly particular to God, it has a kind of infectious quality, which manifests itself simply by being near God. So, for example, at a tangible and physical level, Moses has to remove his shoes at the site of the burning bush because the ground is holy, and because God is present (Exodus 3.5). However, this understanding of holiness is not restricted to sacred places and holy ground. People become holy by proximity too; holiness is seen as a divine quality that God shares. This perspective is taken up in the Christian scriptures. (See, for example, 1 Peter 1.15, 'Be Holy because I am Holy.' And even more particularly, John 17.19, 'I consecrate myself for them that they too may be set apart.')

It is easy to misunderstand the nature of holiness as exclusive and excluding, although the early Christian leaders seem never to have intended that to be so. Far from being an elitist class, Paul describes holiness as a 'calling' for the Christian communities that he founded. These communities were first to be seen as holy simply because they were identified as the new body of Christ. However, they were to see holiness as something they were in the process of becoming, rather than as something they had attained. He described the outward signs of this in what he perceived importantly as a movement from the fruit of the flesh to the fruit of the spirit. All this is done with God's co-operation and grace.

Priestly holiness – set apart for what?

The priestly view of holiness as 'otherness' determines that the 'holy' is set apart for God. In itself this is not a problem. Human beings set things apart in the sense that they put them aside. My grandparents used to talk about saving for a rainy day. The problem with this was that the saving was seemingly an exercise with no purpose. Money was put away and never used. It is clearly unsatisfactory to think of God setting apart in this fashion. So in order to understand what being set apart means we need to ask the question, what do we think we are being set apart for?

When God sets us apart we are doing more than occupying storage space on the shelf of life. We are being set apart for a purpose that can best be understood by seeing it as an initiative by God to then channel the transcendent back into the ordinary and everyday. This moves it on from a static perception to one that has momentum and the capacity to engage. God wants to interact within the order of creation. How does that happen? Seemingly, by channelling the values of the Kingdom in the form of gratuitous love through those who have already caught the message. Why does God want to do that? Well, perhaps in the first instance we might see it as having something to do with our understanding of holiness as health, wholeness and healing. Certainly the word holy has the same root as these other words, and with this insight the gift of holiness becomes God's instrument for mending, changing and transforming a world that bears the scars of human imperfection and has yet to grasp the radical challenge of the Kingdom's values personified in Christ. It is easy simply to see these values as ethical rather than mystical, and to pad around on the ground floor of the kingdom being useful and good, instead of taking the stairs to another level. This would demand a reassessment of how we always looked at things and why; who stands to gain by preserving the status quo and why it is in their interest to do so.

In a very good article on holiness and the saints Sara Maitland tells us that to find out what holiness is we need to look at some of the lives that have been deemed to be holy and then take a second look, as to why they were so.[3] If we want to know something about the radical nature of healing as attested to in the Gospels there is a different way of looking at some of these lives that helps us see something new and dynamic in holy living.

> . . . we cannot be holy, until we have learned to see and understand a history of holiness and to see it in relation to the political and social realities of its different times . . . The particular acts that spring from holiness and may lead to sainthood are bound to be different at different times and in different places . . . Within a European and patriarchal tradition the representation of the marginalized has particular difficulties.[4]

She cites the example of some women saints in the history of Christian hagiography and looks particularly at the classification of virgins. In a culture that was obsessed with female purity, very few women saints are categorized as other than virgins. This tells us a good deal about the collective hagiographical authorship of the lives of the saints as we have received them. In other words a basic feminist reading of this situation tells us not only that those who recorded the lives of the saints were all men, but also that they were men who were content to collude with the social and political framework of the day. The concept of virginity as religious purity was a way of controlling women. Maitland suggests, however, that there is another level at which a feminist reading of this can be applied, and it gives us a completely different angle. She quotes Peter Brown's *The Body and Society*,[5] in which he suggests that the emphasis on virginity in late antiquity was a radical anti-state protest by women. In the absence of contraception, women renouncing sex was interpreted as a refusal to act as a good citizen in an empire with a declining population. This was not primarily about endorsing the dualistic thinking on religious purity, it was a prophetic, eschatological and political act! Holiness, seen this way, means being set apart for change, and being holy means being open to effecting that change.

This radical reappraisal of virginity can be seen at other times in hagiographical history as a depiction of the way in which women retake control of their lives from parents and husbands who treat them as possessions. Ownership of persons in this way is something of an unofficial slavery, controlling and directing the matters of family life in a non-egalitarian fashion. If we think that all of this is a far cry from the principles of the Kingdom as gratuitous love, then we are probably right. Here what the act of embracing virginity does is to counter the perceived injustice of this unofficial slavery by refusing to collude or cooperate with it. It strikes a blow for the values of the Kingdom. Human beings, virgin saints, become agents of change in history, but not primarily because they buy into a sexual purity cult. It is because they show that holiness, that activity of channelling between God's transcendence and God's immanent activity in the world, challenges human social constructs when they emerge to favour one group at the expense of oppressing another.

This 'radical virginity' is the face of another age. In the Western world, with the wide availability of oral contraception, women are able to take control of their lives and its sexual liberty in more ways than by preserving their virginity – though that indeed remains an option. It seems ironic, then, that within the contemporary Church, gay and lesbian clergy now find chastity, in the form of sexual abstinence rather than virginity, imposed upon them. As already outlined, a clear recommendation of *Issues in Human Sexuality* was that although there might be a way of accommodating the open relationships of gay and lesbian couples who were not ordained, this was not an option for those wanting to be ordained. The reason given being:

> Because of the distinctive nature of their calling, status and consecration, to allow such a claim on their part would be seen as placing that way of life on a par with heterosexual marriage as a reflection of God's purposes in creation.[6]

In light of this perception of the withholding of sexual consent as protest, sexual behaviour and social lifestyle might thus be seen as a means of channelling God's values by protesting against those in power. If that is so, we need to ask, are those clergy in openly gay and lesbian relationships responding prophetically to an attitude of power that is itself not embracing the Kingdom concept of gratuitous love?

Holiness as courageous, adventurous and welcoming

It would be very wrong to say that the primary motive for gay and lesbian clergy couples living openly together is that they want to challenge the oppressive and unjust structures of an institutional Church that is not ready to accept them. This is certainly not the reason why these couples found each other in the first place. For most, living with someone in an open, supportive relationship is part of the adventure of life and whatever else we say about the saints of God, most of them have embraced the spirit of adventure.

> I also want to be in a relationship where there is adventure, change and growth, because I think that fundamentally that is what we are here for. I am not here to be the same person at the end of the year as started at the beginning of it, or at the end of my life as at the start. I want to be radically different and closer to what I understand God's holy law to be.
>
> Male priest with partner 6 years

The saints also live courageously. Their traversing back and forth across the holiness of God often invites ridicule and misunderstanding of the way they live, but it always challenges us to look at things again in the light of new insights. These couples plainly love each other. Those who love in this way pay attention to each other and are courageous on behalf of one another. So too the saints pursue a course of life that is loving and courageous (often meeting death on the way). But importantly, they do not simply live unto themselves. Holiness and holy living is infectious in the way it inspires.

> In trying to lead a holy life, I think that we are responsible for trying to see the effect it has on others, even beyond the relationship. It is very easy to think about the two of us, but if a life together is lived in holiness it has enormous impact on those around you.
>
> Female priest with partner 3 years

This is a simple but important insight, particularly so for those of us who inhabit a Western European and North American culture so intent on embracing individualism. We can find traces of this human pattern in some of the most ancient stories of the Bible. The call to holiness is not merely personal. It is not merely about Jesus and me. If all it concerns itself with is my personal salvation then it is probably not a life of holiness at all.

We know that holiness to ancient Israel was a very important concept. Before God even brings the people to Sinai, it says in Genesis, 'You shall be a Kingdom of priests and a holy nation.' What does that mean? It surely means to be a community, which is in relationship with God. That is what it is all about. Holiness begins in the desert place. There are these slaves arriving in the wilderness. They have been called into this existence and there in the desert they encounter this 'other' that they have to have this relationship with. Who has liberated them? They haven't liberated themselves! They were brought out of bondage by God and then they have to form a relationship with God which involves being in relationship with one another. That is the great challenge for all humanity. It is about being human beings in relationship with God and with each other. They are to do what is right and good for and by each other and as a community.

Male priest with partner 3 years

If holiness is not merely a defining of self in relation to God, perhaps we can see it more as how God interacts in creation, and conclude that the holy life can only be identified as a holy life when it is generously shared in community. For one couple this was well depicted in the famous Rublev icon of the Holy Trinity. The three that form the subject of the icon are seated around the table, each connected by touch and sight. The gifts of food in the centre of the table suggest eucharistic hospitality, but the genius of the icon lies in the sense of space in the foreground, inviting whoever contemplates the scene to step into it and share the gifts with this holy community.

You have the three and then you have the space at the table that draws others in and it seems to me that a relationship that is lived in accordance with Christ would be a relationship that gave, not only internally, but also gave to others

*and was a gift to others as that love overflowed. I think that is what we would
be looking for however imperfectly we found it.*

Female priest with partner 3 years

Others endorsed this view. If a sign of God's holiness was revealed in
the commitment of God to community transformation and hospitality, then living openly in the Church was a prerequisite for enabling
that to happen. How otherwise was it possible to live this aspect of
God's holy law? How could one entertain angels if one had to remain
hidden?

*I think that hospitality is a really important part of our life and ministry and
it is also important to say that this doesn't come naturally to us. Actually we
are both quite private people and we would much prefer to be able to shut the
door at the end of the day and live our lives more privately, but I think we both
feel that we are called to reflect God's generosity through our own generosity to
other people. I guess that there is something about a belief that we have that
God is hospitable to us in our partnership and that is about being hospitable
to other people. Having visitors and strangers through the door here is part of
what being a household is about.*

Female priest with partner 2 years

Looked at this way, hospitality is not merely about how much food
one serves on to the plate of a guest, or even the manner in which one
greets a stranger. It is to do with knowing God, which in turn implies
that it concerns how far we are prepared to let people into our lives.
How much of ourselves are we prepared to give away in the hospitable encounter? Does any of this really contravene the 'distinctive
nature of [a priest's] calling, status and consecration'? Does it not,
rather, enable a model of holy living that calls the priest to be an agent
of change in a world God is constantly working in to transform?

Prophetic holiness and political love

Liberation Theology does not enjoy the level of popularity it did in
the closing decades of the twentieth century, but there is no doubt

that it has left a legacy of language and method that enables everyday Christians to participate in the experience of theological reflection. What makes it liberating is that it values the experience of the most disenfranchised. This in turn opens up the Word of God through scripture to those very people. This is not particularly new: for centuries some of the greatest saints and mystics have espoused the interfacing of scripture and experience to aid the discovery of holy living.

Ignatius Loyola, the fifteenth-century founder of the Jesuits, is a good example. He discovered the spiritual life in a new and quite revelatory way when, during a lengthy period of convalescence after a battle, he allowed his imagination and his life experiences to interface with the scripture stories he was reading. By entering the stories of the Bible through his imagination he learned that God's revelation through human experience goes on in every age. Thus the revelation of God in scripture is not doubted, but it shows that revelation does not exist merely in some vacuum of history, but also in the contemporary life of everyday people.

What Ignatius suggests is that our experience is a crucial means through which God goes on revealing himself to us all in every age. What makes this liberating is that taking human experience seriously doesn't diminish the honour we accord the sacred texts, but it changes the way we relate to them. What it enables is a new accessibility. Not only is human experience liberated and given a sense of worth, but the Word of God is liberated from the words on the page. Countless people who have spent their lives describing themselves as 'ordinary' now have access to a meaningful way into the scriptures, expelling what is otherwise close to blasphemy, namely that God couldn't possibly speak to or through them because their life experience is so humdrum and dull. If we can believe that God has a track record of taking and transforming the way we see and make use of these perceived 'ordinary' lives, then in our search for holy living we are forced to look for it in the life of action directed towards the transformation of the unjust social structures that impinge upon those lives. This is a commitment to establish what I call a political love. The starting point of Liberation Theology is a bias towards the poor, those who are at the bottom of the social, economic and religious pile. As they read their lives into scripture, the Word comes alive in the sense that they see that God has always favoured those in places of oppression – like themselves.

I am convinced that how we interpret 'the poor' always emerges from the context we inhabit. So the situation of the poor of South America living in shanty towns within politically insecure infrastructures cannot be directly transposed into the social and political context of Western Europe and North America. However, the revelation of prophetic holiness can be found in these contexts if we access the framework and insights of Liberation Theology.

Political love takes the side of the poor as it sees them and seeks to transform their situation. The poor are the ones with the greatest sense of powerlessness, whose lives are controlled by the directives of those in authority, and when those directives oppress, they are to be resisted without violence. When this occurs we see political love as the fundamental material of prophetic holiness. Some describe this as *kenosis*, a theological term that describes the outpouring of Jesus' self. In this context, it is the descent into the world of the poor in order to unmask and denounce oppression.[7] The resistance to oppression almost inevitably leads to persecution, and in the most volatile places Christians espousing this political love can expect to be attacked, vilified, expelled or even killed. However, the persecution confirms for us that we have been in the presence of the most fundamental love.

While the context the Church inhabits in Western Europe and North America is not one depicted by the shanty town, it nevertheless seems clear to me that it is one that invites discrimination and recrimination of a different kind. Although the Church has begun to address some issues of race and gender, it still maintains benign systems that oppress women, under the guise of preserving the conscience and integrity of those who still, after many years, are unable to accept the priestly ministry of women and the episcopal ministry of the men who ordain them. Currently in England the Church discriminates against any woman who might feel called to serve as a bishop. Few of its senior leadership posts are occupied by minority ethnic groups. But it reserves its greatest portion of oppressive energy for opposing gay and lesbian clergy who want to be as open about their lives and partnerships as their heterosexual colleagues.

This became most publicly visible in the summer of 2003 when Gene Robinson was (openly) elected Bishop of New Hampshire in the Episcopal Church of the USA and Jeffrey John was chosen (through the peculiar secret system of the Church of England) to be Bishop of Reading. Both men are gay and honest about their respective relationships. Both men had already been accorded a degree of preferment within the Church, each a canon of their respective diocesan cathedrals. Robinson lives openly and actively with his partner; John and his partner do not live together and declare themselves celibate. Both men became the object of vitriolic abuse, the worst of which came from within the Church. Robinson had death threats. At the General Convention of ECUSA that year, the presiding bishop, Frank Griswold, reminded those present that Gene Robinson 'is a member of the body of Christ, not a symbol of an issue'.

But this fell largely on deaf ears. It failed to stem the threats from dissenting clergy and their parish representatives to withhold financial contributions to the Diocesan Common Fund of the Diocese of New Hampshire. In England, wealthy parishes in Oxford threatened to do the same. Robinson was duly consecrated; John, under pressure, was asked to withdraw his acceptance, which he did. Within a year some primates of the southern hemisphere were declaring their provinces out of communion with New Hampshire and calling for the expulsion of ECUSA from the worldwide Anglican Communion.

Political love revealing itself as non-violent resistance is not easy to see, at first glance, in the lives of the couples in this sample. Most of them openly declared that 'campaigning' was not really their forte, although they recognized its value and were grateful to those who did. Their resistance was far more low-key, but it revealed a determination not to be subjected to the humiliation of hiddenness that they all saw as debilitating and unhealthy. One couple noted that the propensity of many single gay people was to become unhealthily introverted and introspective. This left them with a depressing choice: either to live promiscuously on the pretext that they couldn't manage the alternative, or to cling to a partner in a secret relationship where all the energy was spent ensuring they were not discovered. It does not take a genius to see that neither of these options is particularly healing or liberating for the couples and the communities they inhabit.

Some described their relationship as a journey, but importantly a journey that took them away from an oppressive past. Often it was one in which they had needed to come to terms with feelings of guilt because of the discovery that they were gay, some of which had been visited on them by the Church.

Certainly as a teenager becoming aware of my sexuality, the guilt was massive and was compounded by the indications of who I was becoming as a sexual person. By that I mean the kind of fantasies I had at the time. As a teenager I was part of the evangelical Christian world and experienced very clear and profound rejection. So the guilt has been a constant, but thankfully diminishing part of my understanding of myself for the last 30 or so years.

Male priest with partner 7 years

The sheer memory of the guilt of coming to realize I was gay is horrible. I never want to return to that way of thinking. When I was a teenager discovering my sexuality, I began to realize that I was different. I heard at school that adolescents go through a phase of homosexual feelings and I began to enjoy myself at that point, feeling that it was perfectly normal. I only began to worry when it didn't seem to pass at about 17 or 18. I don't come from a Christian home, but I had by then become a Christian, baptized as a teenager. So I was developing my faith as well as my sexuality. When it became clear that this was not a phase that I was going through, that was when I began to feel guilty. I felt very dirty at one stage. There came a point when I couldn't go to church and it led me to a nervous breakdown. It was only thanks to the counsel I received from a Christian priest that I came to see that God loved me as I am. God has made me as I am and it was actually blasphemous of me to hate myself in the way that I did.

Male ordinand with partner 8 years

Some tried to make sense of their growing realization that they were different by interpreting it as a particular time of testing and an integral part of God's will and purpose.

When I was considering my vocation that aspect of my life was seen as a burden that although you might have happiness in your relationship, being gay was a burden that actually somehow, being liminal, actually oppressed, was part of God's plan for his priesthood. When I met with, talked to and read the experiences of lesbians and gay men who lived and effectively integrated life, I always found that immensely energizing and empowering and my prayer rejoiced over that.

Male priest with partner 8 years

Others described the complications of family dynamics in which parents and siblings struggled to relate to the changed perception of their child or brother/sister. This sometimes led to the oppression of rejection.

When I was 15 my mother said to me, 'Your father tells me you are gay. You're not, are you?' My dad's attitude was that it was the worst thing that could happen to a man. I grew up with those outlooks and it wasn't until my early thirties that I was comfortable about talking to my friends about being gay. I kept it all very suppressed.

Partner to male priest together 3 years

General social attitudes contributed to the sense of low self-esteem and, in some cases, loathing.

I did have guilty feelings for quite a while, particularly around what is a common perception among people that gay people are somehow quite self-indulgent and self-centred and don't have to think about family responsibilities.

Male priest with partner 20 years

Some found oppressive patterns within the more fundamentalist elements of the Church.

I hooked up with some evangelical Christian friends who took me to several prayer meetings. Here they prayed for me to be healed from my homosexual desires. I even had the great John Wimber pray with me for healing. Funnily enough, I was never cured or healed in that way, and now I feel quite angry with my friends that they disregarded my pain and my integrity and sought to tell me something that they believed. They were utterly judgemental of me and I did feel guilty – yeah! I don't feel guilty any more, though. God made me the way God wanted to make me. The way to holiness certainly won't involve any change in orientation.

Female ordinand with partner 2 years

Others found that this oppression was compounded with what they felt was abusive use of the Bible.

It infuriates me when some people ask me whether I know what the Bible says on the matter. All the way through my training I went through those texts and I still look at them but can see nothing there that can make me feel guilty about what I am. Being gay is what I am and that is what God is taking on and preparing for ordination.

Female ordinand with partner 14 years

One priest testified powerfully to finding healing within the Church. But it came to him in an unexpected fashion, in a way that helped him see what his well-meaning friends in the Church had been trying to do for him.

There was a lot of guilt stuff around in the early days – mainly about sexual activity, but not only that. There was this terrible sense of being dirty or un-acceptable and I certainly heard a lot of sermons and read a lot of books, which said exactly that. What changed all the guilt for me was meeting him. He was the source of the guilt on the one hand but he has become its healer too. Some of my early charismatic experiences, and going forward for healing, I am sure put me into the paths of people who thought they were getting rid of my homo-sexuality, but even though it didn't get rid of it, it did in a funny kind of way underline for me in the experience that God did love me rather than want to shower his wrath on me. God can work – even through that!

Male priest with partner 15 years

Prophetic holiness reminds us that we need always to remain engaged in the political life of Church and world so that political love can remain *love*. Liberating the politically beleaguered should always remain an option open to the Kingdom.

Wisdom holiness, faithfulness and intimacy

The call to holiness which declares the 'otherness' of God and describes this in terms of being set apart could easily be misunderstood as the religious elitism already mentioned, were it not for a third angle from which we are invited to explore it. The whole notion of wisdom holiness demands that we resist the temptation to see or portray holiness too exclusively in a cultic sense because while it sees holiness as something derived from God, this is only in the sense that it is a divine quality to be shared. While it is distinct and different, it is not exclusive to one particular group. We have a good example of this in the Gospels where Jesus is touchingly depicted as one who shares a relationship of intimate quality with God, whom he refers to as 'Abba', the term used by a small child for its father. Holiness, then, in a relational context such as this, while still maintaining a sense of distinctness in the sense of 'other', invites us to see the futility of so exalting God that God's reality is then out of reach. However, to engage in a divine initiative as intimate as this demands the highest level of human response: commitment. Wisdom holiness calls the most radical and authentic holy living out of those pursuing a life of holiness when they affirm, by commitment, the reality of God. To be holy, then, is to be non-autonomous and to be in relation. Proximity to God is not simply a matter of space or ground; it is the reflection of an intimate lifestyle.

Much of Western Christianity has the unfortunate habit of separating belief and practice as if we were still living the Augustinian principle of 'Love God and do as you please'. The gift of intimacy with God, if it is to be reflected through human lifestyles, has to manifest itself in human behaviour. For Christians it is a way of being with God in Christ and not simply an exclusive way of noting our distinctness from the profanity of the secular world. How might we set about understanding this?

Flesh and body

One way we might begin is to attempt a recovery of theological body language. There is no getting away from the fact that the human body is a sexual body, but much of the Christian tradition that is our inheritance seems to be disdainful of the body as a vehicle of sexual expression. The Second Vatican Council was quite clear that holiness was not a term to be harnessed solely by those who had taken vows to explore the Christian faith in contemplative orders, nor by those who were declared members of the Church,[8] yet there remains a cloak of doubt hanging in Christian human consciousness. Are sex and the sacred happy metaphorical bedfellows? I am not sure that they are. So what do we do with the whole Pauline concept of the Church as a body if it is a body that has no sexual expression?

Many would lay the blame for this at the door of the writer of the letters attributed to Paul in the New Testament. He appears to be negative on marriage and sex and is hostile to the body, describing it as something to be subdued. The apparent exhortation that members of the Church should marry if they can't remain sexually chaste (1 Corinthians 7.1) is made ostensibly on the premise that it was better to be practical if they couldn't abstain. It was a safeguard against illicit sex. But we also know that as the Church began to grow in the early centuries of the first millennium, it encountered cultures and thinking that considered the body an inferior dimension of humanness. It was something to be conquered or liberated from. An exhortation like this for a Corinthian church that seems to have been fairly confused about sex and asceticism anyway might lead them to think of sexually active Christians as inhabiting a lower level of spiritual pedigree compared to those practising abstinence.

Pastoral concessions or eternal verities?

Herein lies the real problem in interpreting the sacred texts in relation to contemporary lifestyles. When Paul wrote to the Corinthians, did he really imagine that his one-off pastoral letter to a confused church in unique and complex circumstances would have received the status that has been accorded it by the global Church, with billions of members, 2,000 years later? I somehow doubt it. But in fact this is what has happened. As the sacred texts became part of a developing tradition, that tradition kicked in a way of thinking and being that took the entire Church in a direction that has not served our current search for holy living all that well. From Tertullian, Jerome and Augustine we have the formative influences for much later Christian writing on sexuality and the sacred. Theirs became the monastic model. Other Christian authors rarely argued a case for integrating an active sex life, even in marriage, with a life of Christian holiness. The monastic model renounced sexual pleasure in order to focus on the construction of a religious interior life. While he was involved in sexual activity, Augustine declared that he felt enslaved, driven and compulsive. Devotional manuals that might be of use to lay people not inhabiting monastic orders tended to ignore sexuality or relegated it to the same regrettable category of physical necessity as eating or sleeping. A glance at the works from *The Imitation of Christ* to *The Pilgrim's Progress* bears this out.[9]

Clearly what was happening to the Corinthian church is not happening to us, and therefore if we are to gain from and still find value in the sacred texts we need to look at them in a different light. Thomas Deidun, in an article looking at Paul on sex, reminds us that the apostle distinguishes between flesh and body – something that often escapes our attention.[10] What Paul terms 'flesh' (*sarx*) is not itself sinful, but it is that dimension of ourselves that makes us vulnerable to sin. What we have tended to do in our interpretation of Paul's remarks about 'flesh' is to see them in what Deidun calls a dualistic fashion. We think of flesh and spirit as separate and opposed parts of the self. One is bad and the other good, and the one needs to be subdued by the other. Historically, in the Christian tradition, sex has fallen into the carnal and therefore the 'flesh' category, belonging to the lower part of human nature, needing to be subdued. This is probably not what Paul intended in this pastoral letter, since he had a higher (and non-dualistic) understanding of 'flesh'. He is not talking about a lower nature or sexual disorder, but about the *whole* of us when we resist God. This might reveal itself as sexual disorder, but it might equally reveal itself in a number of other ways that have nothing to do with sex at all. This is made much clearer when we look at what Paul means by the 'body'.

Again, for Paul, the body (*soma*) is not to be seen as just one part of a person. The body is the whole self, both now in its physicality and in any other dimension of human existence. The body is not so much something that we inhabit as what we *are*, and Paul nearly always depicts it as a place of integration with God. The body, he tells us, is for the Lord and the Lord for the body (1 Corinthians 6.13).

It seems that the Corinthians had great difficulty with this kind of body integration, which might have been as a result of the strong cultural influences they inherited from the Greeks, who said that the body was corruptible and an inhibition to the soul. The Corinthians had problems understanding the resurrection, perhaps thinking that it meant no more than the resuscitation of the corpse, and Paul addresses this in chapter 15. But earlier, in chapter 6, Paul challenges the view that they have taken, that sexual activity was something religiously and ethically indifferent. They saw it as functional and no more than that. If the body is a vehicle to be escaped from in favour of a higher order of life, this attitude might be understandable, but by this assertion the Corinthians themselves are falling into a kind of dualism where body is seen merely as a corruptible part of a lower nature. Paul counters this strongly. Because the body is the place of integration with God, thanks to Christ, sexual union should not be seen in such a disengaged way. For Paul, sexual intercourse is significant because it is an act of joining or linking the body with another. However, because of God's work in Christ, when Christians link their bodies in the intimacy of intercourse, it is Christ they take into the sexual encounter, because their body is part of Christ's Body. Paul does not say that they should not engage in sexual intercourse. Instead, he tells them to 'shun immorality!' (1 Corinthians 6.18). Put positively, this might read that they be discerning in the extreme for the sake of the Body of Christ as to with whom they share such sexual intimacy. This is not a licence for free love, even for occasional sex with other consenting Christians, but perhaps it is a directive towards faithful, monogamous relationships. Deidun further suggests that it might be an implicit assent to seeing non-celibate lifestyles as not only compatible with holy living, but enhancing it.

> It is surely capable of a positive development in the context of a God-willed sexual union. For it implies that sexual union can consolidate the union between Christians and Christ in deepening their own union as members of the 'soma'. The theological and pastoral potential of Paul's insight is enormous, even if he himself made no positive use of it.[11]

This is a useful insight in developing a theology of sexuality. An interpretation like this leads us inevitably to an understanding of sexual intimacy in the proper context as a means of gaining greater understanding of God and what it means to live within God. In his letter to the Romans Paul spends the opening chapter chastising them for refusing to glorify God. Ironically, it is this chapter that is most referred to in offering a case against homosexual relations. But it seems to me that the exchange of sexual practices that Paul derides is part of an entire package of practices that the Roman Christians were deploying, which obscured the search for God. They were indulging in sex for the sake of sex and as a consequence they were worshipping the creation rather than the creator. In doing this they were dishonouring the body in the same way as the Corinthians were (Romans 1.25). Their real crime then was that they were risking the disintegration of their relationship with God – a matter of utmost concern to Paul.

There can be little doubt that Paul was committed to celibacy, but if we read his pastoral treatise to the Corinthians with the insights noted here, we might be able to break fresh ground in the quest for holy living and how sexual intimacy might be compatible with that holy living, without having to resort to an imposed celibacy or being unfaithful to the inspiration behind Paul's text.

Sexual intimacy, holy living and a responsibility towards the body was something that all the couples faced up to, though some noted that there was still a tendency within the institutional Church to allocate them separate compartments. Some felt that the integration of sex and the sacred was generally too much for a Church that had historically kept these dimensions apart.

> *Sexual intimacy and holy living are intertwined, even though the Church tries to do a good job of keeping them apart. If they are not linked in a person's life then there is a great diminution in the spiritual life, of energy and imagination. I think that sexual intimacy at its best releases energy and enriches feelings of the self. I think that then blossoms in the spiritual life of prayer and relationships.*

> *Male priest with partner 5 years*

Historically it has served the interest of the institutional Church to attempt to exercise control over the sexual behaviour of its members. Pronouncements on artificial contraception are an example of this. But these pronouncements have also led directly to suffering and misery in overpopulated countries with high levels of poverty. Gay and lesbian couples have experienced a different kind of suppression and control. The homosexual acts as described in the sacred texts of scripture have become in the view of the Church descriptive of all gay and lesbian relationships, and adopted as the justification for prohibition. The guilt that this laid on some couples was very damaging.

> *When we first met we were both unsure as to whether we should be expressing our lives together in a sexual way. I think there was a fair amount of guilt around in the early days, though it is not there now. I am very glad for that.*

> *Male priest with partner 15 years*

Couples whose relationships had been of longer standing found it easier to express their relationship in physical intimacy. As is the case with any couple, they found that as their relationship developed, physical sexual activity took its place within the wide variety of other qualities that marked the maturing of their partnership.

We have a much more relaxed attitude to that side of the relationship. There was a time when it was more active and more important, but the companionship side of our relationship has increased in importance over the years.

Male priest with partner 20 years

For many of the women, sexual intimacy was a principal expression of affection, in which they described feelings of great vulnerability. This description of intimate love was one that many of them used later when trying to describe holy living and how they had gained new perceptions of God.

For me sex is about expressing the deepest feelings that I have for her. So it is important because there are moments of deepest intimacy and the most vulnerable moments. These are the moments when we are most fully ourselves.

Female priest with partner 3 years

For others, the pattern of the relationship they shared most intimately with their committed partner was one that became the model of Christian discipleship they most wanted to adopt. The following of the one became an enhancement of the other

I wouldn't say that it was a prayerful experience or a spiritual experience with a big S, but what it does is that it shows me that I have to be prepared to give. I have to open myself and that is what I have to do with God. Every time, every experience I have of giving myself I am becoming more the kind of Christian I want to be. So for a controlling woman, I am learning to become a very vulnerable one – and that's a word I am learning about. Sex plays a very important part in the way I learn about vulnerability.

Female ordinand with partner 2 years

This vulnerability discovered in the intimacy of a deep and loving relationship was a quality that then enhanced their pastoral care in ministerial life. Quite simply, being loved with tenderness enabled them to exercise a ministry more lovingly and kept them outward-looking, rather than selfishly introspective.

> There is something very profound in sexual intimacy which is about the willingness to be vulnerable in that very private and essential way. This enables me to be vulnerable in the rest of my life and to be more open and intimate (I don't mean physically) in a pastoral setting. The acceptance of each other and our being together is a principal strength which tells me something about how I see God and how I see holy living.
>
> Male priest with partner 8 years

> It can enhance holy living by building up love that can then be outward-looking. After 30 years together I think we have it in perspective and spiritually that is quite liberating.
>
> Male priest with partner 32 years

For some this vulnerability translated itself almost mystically. The tenderness of loving someone with intimate expression was almost impossible to describe. For one person it was akin to (though not the same as) those moments of adoration in the presence of God that could only be wordless. Moments such as when in the presence of the one to whom all hearts are open, all desires known and from whom no secrets are hidden, the terror and beauty of commitment to God was held only by knowing God's assuring love, without being able to describe it. The nearest she could come to it was in the closest moments she shared with her partner.

> This holy living can only be held for me within commitment. As I am committed in my love for God, so this relationship follows the same path. Holiness has a sense for me of being 'clean' before God in the sense of being honest and that is what I feel in those moments of vulnerability and intimate giving that I have with her. When she and I are close like that all that is unspoken or difficult gets wordlessly expressed.
>
> Female ordinand with partner 3 years

146

The Roman Christians Paul addressed were guilty of worshipping the
creature rather than the creator, but there was no such diminishing of
God the creator in the couples who shared their stories with me.
Some were able to articulate new and helpful insights into the nature
of God that had strengthened their discipleship.

For some, the mutuality of their relationship, whether expressed
intimately and privately or lived out together openly in the community, was a reflection of what they understood of God in three persons. This trinitarian relationship, as already mentioned, reveals an
intricate and intimate connectedness of the persons of the trinity.
One couple perceived a link between sexual intimacy, power and
God as creator. Clearly God as creator is the God who has the power
to create. God who becomes incarnate in Jesus becomes vulnerable,
and reflects the creative activity in human living. God as Spirit
empowers the fruit of creation, human beings, to live creatively in
God's vision of the Kingdom.

> Sexual intimacy relates to holy living in two very obvious ways. One is in the
> monogamous relationship that we are committed to living out. The business
> of being mutual within the relationship and within sexual intimacy is also
> important because it is something to do with the equality of power in the rela-
> tionship which I think is derived from some sort of sense of the power that God
> empowers us with. Sexual intimacy is a very profound place of discovery for
> that mutuality of trinitarian theology. It comes in the form of that sense of
> mutual indwelling, of utter closeness with a person which, when expressed
> physically, is incredibly beautiful and not in any sense dirty. It describes the
> goodness of sexual intimacy.

> Male priest with partner 15 years

God the creator, who enters human life in the vulnerability of Jesus
Christ, is the supreme image of self-giving love. This love becomes
the ultimate in the expression of God's holy law and the search for
holy human living.

> I think that the expression of a vulnerable, self-giving love is the deepest
> expression of which as human beings we are capable. It seems to me that part

147

of the way that we reflect our creation in the image of God is by loving in that deep, committed, vulnerable way. The sexual relationship is part of that.

Female priest with partner 5 years

This sentiment was supported unanimously. Everyone was reluctant to adopt a position of imposed celibacy; all saw it as contrary to their calling, some relayed the damage it had done to them, others were explicit that intimate loving in a stable partnership was part of the search for holy living.

I can remember in the early stages of our relationship really praying a lot and praying hard about not so much 'Is this okay?' but 'How am I going to find you God, in this?' We were very clear from the beginning that it wasn't right to separate or compartmentalize all that was happening. Somehow it was all connected.

Female priest with partner 2 years

The search for holy living has revealed an understanding of the trinitarian God that is expressed in mutuality: God that is creative power, the incarnate God who is vulnerable and self-giving, and the mystical God of wordless adoration. We have developed the idea of a sense of being set apart for God and what it is that we are set apart for. Being set apart seems to be less about being put on one side and asked to behave in a less interactive way than the heterosexual component of human creation, and rather more about being a model of faithful living.

Faithfulness is a key theme of God's relationship with Israel in Hebrew scripture. On the issues of faithfulness and unfaithfulness the passion of God is aroused. We find this to some degree in the Torah but much more so in the prophetic writings. The story of Hosea, for example, is quite shocking, as the prophet, through his marriage to a prostitute, enacts the unfaithfulness of the Israelite nation, to draw their attention to God's love and longing for them. This theme is revisited in the Christian scriptures of the New Testament and is most poignantly portrayed in the Gospels as the figure of Christ is received and then rejected. Denial and betrayal become factors for discipleship and have implications for holy living, as Jesus goes to the cross.

What are the issues of faithfulness for holy living in the setting of a loving and stable partnership? In Chapter 7 we will look at some of these: the complications that arise through our varied perceptions of what constitutes faithful living; whether it can be seen differently from within the gay and lesbian relationship; and just how it affects the quest for holy living and the search for God in the wider picture of life.

Notes

1 Donald Nicholl, *Holiness*, Darton, Longman and Todd, 1981, p. 11.

2 *Holiness*, p. 12.

3 Sara Maitland, 'Saints for Today', *The Way*, vol. 36, no. 4, 1996, p. 275.

4 'Saints for Today', p. 278.

5 Peter Brown, *The Body and Society*, Columbia University Press, 1988.

6 House of Bishops, *Issues in Human Sexuality*, Church House Publishing, 1991, 5.17, p. 45.

7 Jon Sobrino, *Spirituality of Liberation – Towards Political Holiness*, Orbis, 1989, p. 82.

8 Michael Downey (ed.), *New Dictionary of Catholic Spirituality*, The Liturgical Press, 1993, p. 487.

9 Margaret R. Miles, *The Image and Practice of Holiness*, SCM Press, 1988, p. 98.

10 Thomas Deidun, 'Beyond Dualisms: Paul on Sex, Sarx and Soma', *The Way*, vol. 28, no. 3, 1988, pp. 195ff.

11 'Beyond Dualisms', p. 203.

7

And this is my solemn vow

HOLY LIVING AND THE PLEDGE TO FAITHFUL COMMITMENT

I am writing this on the feast of Corpus Christi. I have just returned from early morning communion at a small chapel in the centre of the parish. There were only eight of us there, and as I sat in the early morning quiet, with the sun breaking through the chapel windows, I was struck by two particular thoughts.

The first was that of commitment. In the previous chapter, scripture, the Christian inheritance and the experience of the couples taking part all testified to the importance of faithful commitment in the search for holy living. At this communion service it felt that simply being there, at an hour when most people were still finding their way out of bed, was in itself a simple act of faithful commitment to this search.

The early morning mid-week service is a marked contrast to the Sunday offering, which in our church tends to err on the busy side, with lots of activity, involvement and sometimes quite distracting noise, most of which is *not* made by the children! Getting out on a Thursday morning by 8 o'clock is an effort, but once there I find a quiet feeling of space, and a liturgy that moves at a different pace. This sense of space I value precisely because of its contrast, but as to valuing the commitment to being there, what exactly were the eight of us this morning committing ourselves to?

The significance of Corpus Christi is that it names the mystery and reveals the commitment. In any Eucharist, and in the celebration of Corpus Christi particularly, the Body of Christ eats the body of Christ. There is much emphasis on the one feeding on the other, the Body being nourished and sustained by the body, and it cannot be otherwise argued that whatever Christians understand by the body and being in the Body, it is of extreme significance and value. If we are to take our body language seriously then the argument apparently proposed by some of the Corinthians to Paul (see the previous chapter), that what we do with our human bodies has no significance or bearing within the Body of Christ, is simply not sustainable for meaningful contemporary Christian discipleship. If we take a sense of commitment into the Eucharist, because through the powerful signs in bread and wine we glean something of God's commitment to the Body, then we are already participants in the search for what it means to be committed and faithful. What we look for between God and ourselves, we live through our relationships and our life together in the Body.

The second thought occurred at the exchange of the Peace midway through the liturgy. Once again this was in marked contrast to the Sunday scramble in which the parish church momentarily becomes a happy hubbub of Christians all doing their thing in their own way. Some shake hands, some embrace, some wave and others take the opportunity to catch up on the latest gossip. Some selectively kiss, blissfully unaware of the discrimination they are inadvertently fostering. Nearly everyone uses the same phrase: 'Peace be with you.'

This morning the eight of us accidentally converged in the middle of the tiny chapel and simultaneously shook hands across the centre in a Morris dancing formation style. Each greeted the other with either 'The peace of the Lord be with you,' or 'the peace of Jesus be with you,' before returning to our seats for the eucharistic prayer. As I sat down, the body language of the liturgical Morris dancing moment made me smile. What had I really been a part of in that moment?

Since the reintroduction of the Peace into the modern eucharistic rites, many Western Christians who had hitherto existed in a touch-free zone have discovered the pleasure of personal physical contact. At the same time they may have lost sight of what it is they are doing. Whose peace or what kind of peace are we offering the Body at the Eucharist? Does 'Peace be with you' mean the same thing as 'The Peace of the Lord be always with you'? I don't think it does. There is a sense in which we have succumbed to the secular notion that the establishment of peace takes its lead from the diplomatic services. Conflict is met with consensus and compromise. The peace is kept as an absence of visible conflict. There is no fighting, no killing, no protest and no scope for open discussion and in-depth public dialogue. I do not find this kind of peace when I read the Gospels.

The peace of Christ is not one that merely establishes a means of circumnavigating conflict. Its place in the Eucharist is a powerful enactment of the very Kingdom that we have been exploring in these chapters. At a local level, the declaration of Christ's peace by the Body of Christ is a commitment to finding signs of the Kingdom in the life of our local community. It is not intended to be just talk; it is designed to challenge action. The Peace that we are challenged to bring to the Body is a peace that addresses the issues we face in our communities, things that we confront daily.

As a curate, I served for a short time in a parish in Hampstead where its outgoing Member of Parliament once declared that the people of the constituency suffered from what he called 'Afghan-istanism'. The then Soviet Union had invaded Afghanistan and many of the locals had organized or been part of political protest groups. There was nothing wrong with that in itself, but the constituency then was also reckoned to have the highest suicide rate of anywhere in the country. The MP's point was a pertinent one and showed up something that Christians are often guilty of. The poor belong else-where, and usually as far away as possible. If we can concentrate hard enough on what is over there and far away, we will effectively screen what is in front of our noses, or declare that, by comparison, their need is less and not worthy of our attention.

This was the attitude that was voiced at the Lambeth Conference in 1998. The human sexuality issue (which was shorthand at that conference for the homosexuality issue, despite all attempts to get participants to see it was about them as well as gays and lesbians) was, we were told, time-consuming. It was deflecting attention from 'more important' issues. Somehow being gay or lesbian has become equated with decadent western culture and in the Church in Western Europe and North America is depicted as a sign, if not a cause, of the

Church's demise. Indeed, episcopal voices from parts of the African continent have described it as evidence that the Church is under satanic attack.[1] Despite the 1998 Conference resolution to listen to the experiences of gay and lesbian people, there appears to have been little commitment to this from those who passed it and in some cases an apparent determination to prevent any from trying.

Perhaps we should not be surprised at this, or too scornful. The Peace of Christ is supposed to be a transforming peace, and it is often best seen when it emerges from within the experience of a local community trying to live out the signs of the Kingdom as gratuitous love. That local experience needs time to be assimilated at other levels within the Church. This process of assimilation invariably moves through the unfortunate but seemingly necessary phases of misunderstanding or mistrust, of defensiveness and the impact that a growing sense of understanding in a different way brings. In talking about committed gay and lesbian relationships and the attempts to live lives of holiness, we all find ourselves starting from different places and with individual understandings of what that means. What I have tried to do here is to give safe space to the experiences of some clergy and lay people so that you might read and reflect for yourself. But this is no substitute for experience at first-hand. I regret that because of the current climate, everyone participating has to remain nameless. While it may be that for now this is the only way, it is clearly not a satisfactory state of affairs that members of the Body of Christ have to remain hidden because they fear discrimination and retribution. What kind of peace is that?

Body language and worship

The Peace of Christ is placed liturgically immediately before the preparation of the eucharistic gifts. The act of reconciliation in the Anglican rite demands the transformation of heart before propelling us into the mystic poetry of the eucharistic prayers. The Body prepares to worship the body before the intimacy of communion. In a culture where we tend to idolize the body, some recovery of authentic Christian body worship would not go amiss.

With my body I thee worship . . .

What did Archbishop Cranmer mean to convey when he wrote these powerful words into the vows of his Order of Service for the Solemnization of Matrimony? If nothing else, he has given us an implicit understanding of the Divine, by confronting us with an explicit expression of the human, even if we have sadly watered down 'worship' to 'honour'. It is in the closeness of a relationship intimately expressed as sexual union that we most commonly find the language of faith, either consciously or inadvertently expressed. As some of those surveyed have already testified, the most intimate language of love is that of adoration, but it does not exist in a vacuum. Adoration, which we readily need no translation for in the language of romantic human love, somehow becomes an embarrassing word for many Christians when moved across to the religious language column. Worship suffers the same fate. I suggest that it is only in opening up what people mean when they express the language of faith, worship and love in their human relationships that it becomes possible to recover a confidence to see, name and express the same of, and in, God.

If the act of Eucharist is about how the Body of Christ meets the body of Christ, then I think we can conclude that the physical human body is important to God. What we do with it in relation to other human beings and to God is important, too. It is in the language of worship and love that we find the best opportunities to express this. Most of us have an acute sense of what we think love is and many of us might say we have experienced it in some form or another. Grasping a sense of worship and an understanding of what that is tends to be more difficult for a Western Church obsessed with a culture of entertainment and dogged with the accusation that what passes for worship in its churches is simply boring. Yet I am convinced that it is within a context of worship generally, and eucharistic worship particularly, that Christians can make the best sense of what they understand the relationship of worship and love to be. I am convinced because it seems most naturally to draw together those values of the Kingdom that emerged at that early morning Holy

Communion on the feast of Corpus Christi, namely a sense of commitment and the search for the Peace of Christ.

Lives of faithful commitment

The problem with faith is that some Christians confuse it with the language of certainty. A few years ago Anne Atkins, a freelance journalist, appeared on a satellite channel talk show in which she complained about clergy who expressed doubts, describing them, as I recall, as self-confessed atheists. But faith is the opposite of certainty and the reality of faith is that it co-exists with doubt. That is also the reality of how most of us have to live our most significant human relationships. The desire for faithfulness is in itself an aspect of faith and it is coupled ideally with a sense of trust. In the written language of the New Testament this is well shown. The Greek word *pisteo* is the same root word for the English words faith, belief and trust, and in writings like the fourth Gospel they are almost interchangeable. While we might like to think that there was certainty in our human relationships, they probably wouldn't be human if there was. What is realistic is the way that couples have to work at building trust if they are to enhance a sense of faith in each other and the relationship they have committed themselves to.

For some of the couples who had been in relationships of two decades or more, the possibility of living openly at the beginning of the twenty-first century was still something of a novelty. Their relationships, which had begun in their youth, at the outset had involved much secrecy. It was an oppressive context and not one enabling of sound, healthy openness.

> Certainly when we were young, you couldn't go out and have a boyfriend and build up a relationship. Anything that happened would be furtive. So gay people were used to casual meetings back then. In those days, society applauded when one boy publicly went out with one girl, but with gay men (I can't speak for lesbians) it wasn't possible. That's how gay life was. So because of all that it was quite easy to fall into what you might term infidelity.

> Male partner to priest together 32 years

This gives us an important insight into how difficult it is to attain a faithful partnership if the cultural environment in which it is set is not sympathetic to that style of partnership, and even conspires to work against it. If there is any truth in the ongoing accusation from some parts of the Church that gay and lesbian people's lifestyles are promiscuous and their relationships fleeting, then perhaps we should ask whether, as a Church, we bear some responsibility for that. A failure to supply the social infrastructures and liturgical rituals to support couples and enable them to live openly could be seen as a tacit collusion with the rebellion that perpetual promiscuity (mistakenly, in my view) declares itself to be. While there is always the possibility that relationships might be temporary, as we explore them in their initial phases, this is not ultimately the reflection of holy living for a holy lifetime that we are seeking.

This man and his priest partner now enjoy a degree of openness that was not available for them 30 years ago. Theirs is a monogamous success story (though there are perhaps many more that were not), which was partly due to a thawing in the attitude of the Church at a local level where they were now identified as a couple. This is not an unusual dynamic in the way the institutional Church embraces change. Rarely does a change in attitude occur from the top down. The admission of children to communion, the marriage of divorcees, lay training, women's ministry, church planting, the Alpha course and the blessing of same-sex unions – all started as local initiatives that took the experience of the local church community seriously. It is only later that such issues came to be considered to become national Church policy.[2]

Other couples, too, saw their relationships as 'emerging' in the Church's consciousness, and this affected what they understood by faithfulness within the relationship. Many felt that faithfulness was often treated as a condition imposed to give some kind of regulation to the relationship. This was unhelpful, particularly given their understanding that faithfulness emerges from faith. Regulations, like vows, emerge from and give description to the relationship as it grows. In other words it was a sign of the relationship and how healthy it was.

It has always seemed to me that either the relationship is working or it is not. In that sense the level of intimacy experienced within it might be an important indicator of how that relationship is. In which case it is better to know than not to know. When he and I began our relationship it was never an imposed condition. However, as the relationship has gone on I have no doubt whatsoever that we have both been faithful and the longer the relationship goes on the more I feel that to be the case. So for me fidelity is something that emerges and confirms the rightness of our 'marriage'.

Male priest with partner 8 years

Seen this way, faithfulness has the positive sense of confirming something in the relationship rather than the negative implication of what the relationship may not do or be. Others thought that there was rather more to it than that. Faithfulness might be something that emerged from the relationship in practice, but it was partnered with the whole phenomenon of commitment, which lent itself in some publicly acknowledged form. This is a widely recognized virtue in the Church's different liturgies. The established rites of baptism, confirmation, ordination and marriage all require personal commitment in a public setting. Yet the Church continues to withhold similar endorsements for gay and lesbian couples from its national policy. Indeed, as already seen, at the behest of some parts of the Anglican Communion, pressure has been brought to bear on local initiatives where a congregation or diocesan forum has attempted to create pastoral liturgy to support such couples. Most of the couples in the sample had either made a public commitment, or wanted to, or had undertaken some kind of 'informal' promise-making with their partner.

While public ritual is no talisman for success in a marriage or other kind of committed partnership, it does express openly a desire for wholeness and integrated living under God. For some couples it was an important sign in their search for order and stability. Public commitment is never an easy thing to do, and the lack of social infrastructure and liturgical ritual support creates an environment of uncertainty which feeds insecurity, and can manifest itself in the dark and destructive face of infidelity. This is not unique to gay and lesbian couples but there were some who had lived through the experience of unfaithfulness and described the chaos and damage that ensued.

> I went to a party and made a decision after several drinks and being pursued that I would sleep with the hostess. And I thought, as I wrestled with myself over whether I could do it or not (my partner was travelling, as she did quite frequently with her work), 'People do this all the time. It's all right; it's not going to change my life.' But what I didn't have any idea about was how it would devastate me on a soul level. I had no idea that I was the kind of person who could do that – who could betray a person who had given me everything. It destroyed us both and it took me five years to recover. I had to deal with who I was and what I had done and it did utterly devastate me. I would certainly never put myself in that position again.
>
> Female ordinand with partner 4 years

Others told of how sexual infidelity led to an erosion of the relationship in aspects that were irretrievable. It was impossible to split the different aspects of the relationship.

> I have experienced infidelity with another and there it was less the sex and more the lying that mattered. The dishonesty that it brought on led to a kind of living a double life. So I think that we have both been sufficiently hurt by other people's untrustworthiness in the past that it has made it so important to us now.
>
> Female priest with partner 2 years

Nearly every couple interviewed had discovered the value of commitment and the desire for faithfulness with their partner. What was interesting was that all the women saw sexual fidelity and affectionate intimacy as synonymous. Most of the men did too, but some indicated that a case might be argued in which some wider sexual activity and the sense of still being faithful in a partnership with one person might be possible.

That is something that a lot of heterosexual people don't understand; that sex with a small 's' is not a threat. It can be part of maintaining a friendship. We had a theology and sexuality discussion workshop in the diocese and it was one of the real sticking points among heterosexual people there that our view on this particular matter (the gay point of view) is entirely different.

I think it is to do with heterosexual sex being tied up with the procreation of children. Sex isn't to be seen as the consummating sense of ownership.

Male priest and partner together 20 years

The argument seems to be that on matters pertaining to sexual behaviour even the most liberal-thinking heterosexual is part of a collective mindset that has already drawn the ethical map based upon heterosexual perceptions and assumptions. This is a challenging accusation, but how true is it? It is certainly true that the public debate on gay and lesbian relationships and life in the Church has forced everyone else to look again at what sexual intimacy means for all of us. When the Bishop of Carlisle appeared on national television declaring that 'It's, well, in a way obvious that the penis belongs with the vagina and this is something fundamental to the way God made us . . .',[3] he inadvertently did the whole discussion a massive service. To be fair to him, he was only saying openly what many people think privately. But perhaps more important, by saying it publicly his sentiments came across as embarrassingly oversimplistic. To reduce the intricacy of human sexuality and all that goes with it to the functional operation of our body apparatus is woefully inadequate. That we could have thought that way for so long is simply not good enough if we are to define a theology of sexuality worthy of the name. But, of course, it supports the assertion that only the male heterosexual perspective has ever been considered in the formation of ethical sexual behaviour, and so this debate now forms part of a wider debate to challenge that perspective. In other areas of human sexual behaviour, women have found a voice to describe changes of attitude and perspective.

Within Christianity, and it is not just there, but within our whole culture, sex is generally understood as a penis entering a vagina. But if we understood sex as Christ drawing creation to himself then we have to question the status of that particular act.[4]

The formerly held view that sexual intercourse was solely for the procreation of children is not one now espoused by mainstream Christian Churches. Participation in the creative activity of God is no longer seen as one that is authentic only if it produces children. Similarly, the view that sexual consummation implies a personal possession of the other (usually the man of the woman) is no longer a seriously sustainable perception in Western European culture, and is reflected by the Church in the greater sense of mutuality that it accords partners in its marriage rite. Whether the modelling of that rite finds its way into the marital relationship is another matter.

Rowan Williams, in his essay, 'The Body's Grace',[5] suggests that what we might be learning is that our loving through the body is putting us back in touch with a sense of desire and joy.

For my body to be the cause of joy, the end of homecoming, for me it must be there for someone else, be perceived, accepted, nurtured; and that means being given over in the creation of joy in that other, because only as directed to the enjoyment, the happiness, in that other does it become unreservedly loveable. To desire my joy is to desire the joy of the one I desire.[6]

So with these counter-opinions in mind, I am not sure what sex with a small 's' really means. Regardless of which sexual perspective brings it to the discussion, I can't seem to square what I think it might mean with this description of bodily joy. This description propels us far beyond the idea that sex between consenting adults is acceptable so long as it does no harm. The language of joy and desire belongs with the language of adoration and worship precisely because it is a language that expresses itself intimately. But Williams reminds us that the discovery of joy means something rather more than the bare facts of sexual intimacy. Relationships are not passive and we are not to be passive instruments to each other. Relationships need to take time to grow in fullness.[7]

Furthermore, as we have already seen, relationships do not exist in isolation. Those who live in community or with community responsibility know that what they do and how they are has a ripple effect, impacting on everyone else within that community. For Christians living in the Body this is particularly so. When the Body has a worldwide dimension, understanding differences as we learn to relate to each other will take a lot of time.

The threat of dualism has already received some attention. In Chapter 6 we saw how the Corinthian Christians had misunderstood what it meant to live as the Body of Christ because they had a poor perception of their physical human body. They treated their bodies as mere apparatus and if they were indulging in sexual promiscuity then it was because their attitude towards sex was one of indifference. Sex was merely something that one did – a function of the body.

Paul is annoyed with them not simply because they are behaving in an immoral fashion, but because they are guilty of dualistic thinking and this has carried over to their behaviour. The physical human body does not lead them into any knowledge of the divine nature, so the body doesn't matter to them and is not accorded the same dignity and regard as what they consider their higher human selves to be. The problem with the idea that sex is all right if it does no harm is that it appears to fall into something akin to this category of thinking, for it suggests either that bodily intimacy can be kept separate from feelings of desire, or that it somehow has no bearing on the rest of the Body of Christ. Even some of those who had suggested that sex with a small 's' might be possible expressed uncertainty with the first view. They were anxious not to appear demanding or dependent, but almost all said that they would be hurt and confused if they discovered that such an encounter had taken place. Whatever else it did, for most it was activity that had the potential to sow the seeds of doubt.

It is an area that is difficult in terms of trust. How does that fit in with how one is trying to live a holy life?

Male priest with partner 7 years

The second view, that this would have a negative impact on the Body of Christ, was something none of the participants had considered. And how many of us ever do? Yet it is clear to Paul, who has a highly developed model of Church when he speaks of it as the Body of Christ, that this is what is principally wrong with the Corinthians' attitude. What individuals do affects the whole Body, because in becoming the new creation that he describes, membership of the Body means being as Christ in the present. So, all that they will ever do from the moment of conversion and baptism onwards is no longer just as 'self'; it is 'self' as Christ. Thus the Body mattered for Paul and clearly it matters still in our own age. We know this from the varying attitudes of the different parts of the worldwide Anglican communion to same-sex couples, and especially clergy. What one part of the Body does has an impact on other parts of the body. The establishment of pastoral rites for blessing same-sex couples in Canada finds reaction in Nigeria. This is nothing new, as one couple pointed out.

> I think that fidelity is an extremely important aspect of living a moral Christian holy relationship. That is an important part of Christian tradition and yet that is one of the things that is most aggravating in this current furore [the case of the Bishop of Reading and the Bishop of New Hampshire]. All those African bishops who have special permission for polygamous relationships within the Christian community. I think it is an outrageous double standard.

> Female priest with partner 14 years

She has a point. In the Lambeth Conference of 1988, the dominant issue under the umbrella of human sexuality was not gay and lesbian relationships, but polygamous marriages. It is true that same-sex relationships were discussed, but there was no resolution or voting since it was deemed that the Conference was in no position to make any recommendations of the kind it found itself doing ten years later. With hindsight this seems to have been a wise move, particularly in light of the way that the Conference resolved the matter of polygamous marriages within the Christian community.

The African bishops appealed to the 1988 Conference to take account of the significantly different contexts in which they lived, where polygamous marriages occurred. In parts of the African continent such marriages were shaped by a culture that was itself subject to social and economic constraints. Society in general was still largely patriarchal with agrarian economies and a way of life that though quite poor would have clearly defined social status. Polygamous marriage was a reflection of that. The 1988 Conference openly asserted that culture and context did make a difference when seeking to determine a pastoral response. The Conference simply could not legislate in such an instance. Nobody threatened anybody with excommunication or severed financial links. North American Anglicans neither condemned it as a satanic attack, nor did it become the adopted culture of their dioceses. Instead, those different parts of the Communion decided that it was time to take time. The Body's joy was a loving gesture from different parts of the Body unable to understand the effects of a sexual ethic borne out of a context entirely alien to their own, but prepared to take time to try.

It seems to me that it is possible to apply the insights gained from this consideration for polygamous marriages to the whole business of how same-sex couples, priests and lay people, are met and held within the Church. If the Body matters then it is apparent that we have to do rather more than make threats of excommunication or financial severance, and impose celibacy on a significant proportion of the worldwide Body of Christ. For the Body to follow this path shows a kind of dualistic expression, where one part of the Body considers other parts to be inferior and expendable. One part of the Body holds a high regard for itself while despising another. The call to excommunication, financial severance or imposed celibacy are all signs of that, whereas the attempts to understand how different Christians try to live out lives of holiness within the Body by taking time to understand what that means (as with polygamous marriages) does not. Thanks to African Christians and their appeal for understanding, what Lambeth 1988 does for everyone is to offer hope beyond Lambeth 1998, for it indicates that there is a way of dealing with these difficult issues in a global communion.

From dualism to integration

Paul might have been right to vilify the Corinthian Christians for their inclination to dualistic thinking, but the problem was not uniquely theirs. The temptation to dualistic thinking about the body, and therefore the Body, has been with us in successive generations. Much of this is due to our generally poor view of the physical human body. Some of this has been brought about by a poor appreciation for a theology of creation and a general misunderstanding in Western Christian history of Christian asceticism. The word 'asceticism' simply means discipline, but it has come to be associated with denial and subjugation of the human body to such an extent that it has promoted the path of dualism, the body becoming alienated from the self.

All Christians are called to be ascetics in the proper sense of the word, and we need to recover some of the positive features of that idea, moving away from the negative disparagement of the human body in certain devotional manuals. This view of asceticism is completely at odds with the received doctrines of creation and the incarnation, which emphasize the goodness and integrity of physical living.[8] These doctrines should act as benchmarks for those aspiring to the holy life and the ascetic discipline of Christian discipleship, but too often they have been lost from view in the zealous search for distinction between divine mind or spirit over inadequate body.

Historically, ascetic practice seems to have cultivated this search in the company of fasting and chastity. This is not in itself a bad thing. The purpose behind such practices was to come to a better understanding of the self and to create a greater capacity in the self to love God. Augustine of Hippo made the connection between physical hunger and spiritual longing, and this connection was open to maintaining a positive understanding of these doctrines. The theory behind this is that the temporary abstinence of food and sexual activity had the positive intention of allowing the disciple to become more focused in their senses, on the principle that if those senses habitually became overused they became lazy. So 'resting' them through temporary fasting and abstinence, periods of silence or of solitude, helped renew them. This would appear to be a positive motive for fasting and abstinence. Today there are many who have come to discover enormous value in 'getting away from it all' through making a retreat.

However, it seems that it was not long before most ascetic practitioners came to regard such abstinence as a practical means to elevating the spiritual over the physical. The human body became an enemy needing to be subdued and asceticism became defined as monastic, rigorous and negative. Christian tradition gave birth again to the same dualism that the Corinthians had been guilty of, only this time it was not simply disregarding the body as merely functional apparatus, it was the rigorous control of it through abstinence in order to emphasize the superiority of the spiritual soul over the physical body. Historically this seems to have led the Christian ascetic tradition towards becoming obsessed with its own practices at the expense of the original vision and purpose. Asceticism, far from being something practised by all Christians, became at best elitist or at worse abusive. Such a poor attitude to the human body can only have repercussions of the same kind when dealing with the Body – as Paul argues to the Corinthians. The temptation to dualism remains very hard to shake off.

Ironically, it could be argued that dualism has influenced the House of Bishops' statement *Issues in Human Sexuality*. The suggestion that faithful same-sex relations in the laity might be supported within the Christian community, but not those of the clergy, comes very close to it. The clergy are not recommended to embark on such relationships due to the distinct nature of their calling, or as one member of the House stated, 'because they are the shop window of the Church'. What does this mean? Does this make the clergy part of a higher nature of the Body? If so, what does that imply? Does it mean that it is all right for gay and lesbian lay Christians to have faithful sexually intimate relations because their calling as Christians is somehow less within the Body of Christ than that of the clergy? Are *all* celibate Christians part of a higher calling? The Bishops' directive, doubtless intended to hold the different parts of the Body together, simply creates chaos and confusion by translating a dualistic view of the human body into a dualistic view of the Body of Christ. What they prescribe as pastoral action is in fact the imposition of an ascetic rigorism that, as we have seen, is a corrupt interpretation of its original intention. This directive, then, is no less than the encouragement of bad practice. It makes no sense at all. On the one hand it might continue to imply a 'higher' way of Christian discipleship – through the denial of bodily joy, the gay or lesbian priest can discover an authentic path to holiness. Well, that might be true if the pitfalls of ascetic rigorism as described could be avoided, but it would then be true for anyone. On the other hand it is not a practice which that part of the Body so keen to impose it on gay and lesbian clergy is equally keen to adopt for themselves in their own pursuit of holy living! That being so, one has to question the pastoral integrity of the recommendation.

Towards a deconstruction and Practical Theology

The integrity of this recommendation has to be questioned because there is nothing to show how its implementation might benefit both the clergy and the whole Church. Were the recommendation made out of a sense that all clergy, and particularly gay and lesbian clergy, would grow in holiness, there might be something to be said for it. But it comes across as a compromise, an attempt to throw sufficient crumbs in all directions to keep everyone quiet. This is the kind of diplomatic peace discussed and dismissed earlier as not reflecting the working out of the peace of Christ.

Part of the problem is that the entire Church has accepted one received tradition of human sexuality and human spirituality that has become confused and unsatisfactory for the needs of the Church in our own age. It has explicitly condemned dualism while implicitly fostering it. Historically, the celibate life has often been admired and regarded as a superior calling, and although marriage has been praised as a strenuous spiritual discipline,[9] the Christian tradition does not provide any real apologia of the sexual relationship as a means of self-understanding, of interdependence in relationships, of spiritual growth or of understanding God. Indeed there is evidence to suggest that the influence of Augustine, who declared that in the resurrection there would be sexes but not sex, that we would have bodies with organs but not for use, not only prevailed in its own right, but at the expense of any who dared to suggest otherwise.

> At the end of the fourth century, the British monk Jovinian was excommunicated and anathematized for saying that, for progress in Christian life, marriage was an equally viable life style with celibacy. Both Augustine and Jerome wrote treatises against him, and their treatises remain while Jovinian's writings were destroyed and disappeared. The ascetic excitement of the time partly accounts for the severity of his contemporaries' judgement against Jovinian, but his teaching was not only condemned and suppressed in his own time.[10]

It is clear that the sexual relationship has not been perceived as one in which growth in the spirit, self-understanding and knowledge of God are at all possible. What might have been a prophetic tract for the times was not only silenced but obliterated, and while it might be interesting to ask why, there is insufficient space here to do justice to a subject that others have already given some attention to.[11]

Instead I want to offer some practical ways to advance this discussion. In the world of scholarship, theologians often speak of the need for a deconstruction. As I understand it, this takes apart a previously given theological understanding of a subject when there might be sufficient reason to suppose that the insights it once offered are no longer adequate or complete. Given the dramatic exclusion of Jovinian in his day, and the similar calls in our own day for exclusion of gay and lesbian ordination candidates and bishops who ordain them, I think that we have grounds enough for a deconstruction of the body and the traditionally received perceptions we have of it for the life of holiness we are seeking.

Us and them

Key to the deconstruction is where we each place ourselves in it. So often, theology seems to be done at observable arm's length and this is particularly so in the discussion on theology and human sexuality.

The subject is 'them', and they are not 'us'. What happens to 'them' might be interesting but has no effect on us because they are not 'us' (see Chapter 5). Recently a new bishop was appointed to a diocese in England and he was asked at the usual press conference where he stood on homosexuality. He replied that he stood behind the House of Bishops' report and study guide, but he believed it was very import-ant to encourage *both sides* in listening and 'recognizing the faith of Christ in each other'.[12] This is a very revealing if carefully constructed statement, for it implies no personal involvement or responsibility other than as a facilitator. This has happened time and again in this discussion. We create a two-sided argument and then opt out. This is not about us, it is about them, and our only responsibility is to try and understand them. It is at this point that we fail dismally, for the human body, sexual relations and life together as the Body of Christ is not about 'us' and 'them', it is about all of us.

In the world of modern scholarship we are much indebted to the feminist critique, and in the whole area of asceticism and Christian spirituality this critique has exposed a dangerously one-sided view of sex and attitudes to the human body. A Western Christian tradition that is dominated by an almost entirely monastic male authorship has left a historical legacy that aligns the body with corruption, sin, sex and death. Usually woman is the perceived cause and the pre-scribed remedy is submission of the body through sexual abstinence. The result has been bodily deprecation and self-loathing. If ascetic practice has left us with a poor view of the human body, is there any chance of returning to some of those original insights and recovering them for use in our time? Some would say not, and many supporting the feminist critique would say neither is it desirable. I am not so sure.

If, for example, originally fasting from food or sexual relations were understood as a means of heightening the bodily senses, that would suggest them to be good practices and the bodily senses wor-thy of such attention for their own sake. So we can deconstruct the damaging negative attitudes that emerged towards the body and begin a reconstruction that establishes itself with the original positive insights. The self-denial of abstinence exists only to enhance that which we are already agreed is good, not because something else is in need of suppression. The practices that enable this enhancement then see the human body affirmed and the phenomenon of ascetic practice restored to a positive discipleship, which can be accessed by all. Theologically, the goodness of creation and incarnation can be reborn into this positive view of the body, which is then celebrated (as we celebrate creation and incarnation and resurrection) rather than subdued to the point of abuse.

Fasting as listening

Recovering the affirmation of the body in this way might then enable us to translate some of that positive reconstruction towards the way we live as the Body of Christ. For example, the now positive ascetic practice of fasting (as I have argued it), designed to sharpen the senses, benefits the body, but how will that benefit the Body of Christ? I would suggest that such benefits would be found (senses enhanced) in the way that the different parts of the Body might then deal with each other. As things currently stand, when I look how different parts of the Body of Christ act, I often see what I perceive to be fasting before deconstruction. In other words their 'fasting' is one in which they impose silence in order to gain submission from those parts of the Body with which they disagree. Their goal is not really to listen, but to prevail. Theirs is a negative and destructive fasting that despises other parts of the Body. Suppose instead we treat listening as fasting, from a reconstructed position, and apply it to the subject under discussion, namely the way gay and lesbian Christians, clergy and lay people, live openly in faithful partnerships and strive for holiness. What might this offer?

If the whole Body of Christ, through the resolution of its bishops at the 1998 conference, has pledged itself to listen to gay and lesbian experience of life, then it will need to employ a different kind of listening, a rigorous one that heightens the senses for a time. They will need a deconstructed and reconstructed fasting of listening, a new ascetic.

Perhaps the most respectful listening will be found in the fasting of silent listening. A commitment to respectful listening that is truly meaningful might mean fasting from the immediate retort, the defensive soundbite, the emotive reaction, and instead give measured time to absorbing the full effects of what is being said. A temporary renunciation of the right to talk back might allow time for the voices of the inner heart to have their say. Why do I feel hurt by these people? What is it about them that makes me keep my distance? What is it about me that keeps me from wanting to know them? Proper fasting was one of the features that the Gospels ascribe to authentic deliverance ministry (Mark 9.29). In the fasting of silent listening we might find that some of the fears that appear to destabilize the faith we have grown into might be revealed as nothing of the kind.

That sort of person

In his book *The Church at War* Stephen Bates documents the reactions of the different parts of the Anglican Communion to the appointment of Jeffrey John as Bishop of Reading in the summer of 2003. Among the less dramatic is the account of Mrs Staples, whose husband is vicar of the benefice in which the new bishop was to have resided.

> Among other communications was one from the wife of John Staples, the vicar of Tidmarsh, the little village outside Reading where the suffragan bishop had his residence. Staples himself had made it clear that he was not happy about the appointment, but his wife went somewhat further. She wrote a letter to Dr John saying that, unlike his predecessors, he would not be welcome to park his car on the vicarage drive . . .[13]

In its preview of the book, a journalist from the *Guardian* decided to follow this up.

> 'Yes, well,' she said indignantly, when I rang her up to ask about this, 'that's not the sort of person one wants to meet in one's drive in the morning, is it? It was nothing personal – after he stood down I wrote again and invited him to dinner, and do you know, he's never replied.'[14]

Of course, it makes hilarious reading and Mrs Staples becomes the figure of fun that we all like to point the finger at, but like a lot of comedy, it provides the mask to a tragic darker side. What makes this tragic is the knowledge that Mrs Staples is not alone. There are countless others who think in the 'that sort of person' pattern and for this reason I think we need to pursue a new ascetic within the Body, of silent listening. I hope that the outcome of such a listening will lead at very least to a dawning realization that 'that sort of person' is really no more than a reflection of ourselves and that it has always been so. And I hope that such a deconstruction will move us on in our understanding of human relations, from the lining up of 'both sides' – poofters and lezzos against Taliban-tendency evangelicals – towards something rather more wholesome and honest. To quote Bonhoeffer again, 'We should listen with the ears of God that we may speak the Word of God.'[15]

When we live together in the Body, we are 'that sort of person'. I began this chapter with the rather glib assertion that meeting the body of Christ in the Body of Christ told me something about the nature of commitment. However, it is in the discovery of a reconstructed ascetic insight that I am challenged with what this demands of me. Whenever I kneel within the Body and receive the body I do so alongside thousands of Dr Johns and Mrs Staples. That is the company that I am committed to and amongst whom we all make our search for holy living.

Notes

1 Stephen Bates, *A Church at War*, I. B. Tauris, 2004.
2 Malcolm Torry, *The Parish*, Canterbury Press, 2004, p. 9.
3 BBC Newsnight, quoted in *A Church at War*, p. 167.
4 Jo Ind, in Gordon Lynch, *Losing My Religion*, Darton, Longman and Todd, 2003, p. 69.
5 Rowan Williams, 'The Body's Grace' in *Theology and Sexuality*, ed. Eugene F. Rogers Jr, Blackwell, 2001.
6 'The Body's Grace', p. 313.
7 'The Body's Grace', p. 315.

8 Margaret R. Miles, *The Image and Practice of Holiness*, SCM Press, 1988, pp. 95ff.
9 See Clement of Alexandria, 'Stromaties 3' in *Alexandrian Christianity*, ed. Henry Chadwick, Philadelphia, Westminster Press, 1954, p. 138.
10 *The Image and Practice of Holiness*, p. 99.
11 *The Image and Practice of Holiness*, p. 100.
12 *Church Times*, 9 July 2004, p. 2.
13 *A Church at War*, p. 169.
14 'Canon Fodder', *Guardian*, 20 June 2004.
15 Dietrich Bonhoeffer, *Life Together*, SCM Press, 1972, p. 76.

8

Face to face

People who speak and write within the Christian perspectives should turn our attention to interpretations of Christianity that emphasize love for the goodness and beauty of the created world, the equality of lifestyles in providing the circumstances within which a Christian loves God by – not instead of – loving other people...[1]

A different kind of listening

Having affirmed a commitment to the Body of Christ, rediscovered positive attitudes to the human body that inform us as Church in our own age, and reminded ourselves of the pledge to listen to the voices of the Christian gay and lesbian experience, it seems reasonable now to get on with the business of listening – but in a new and different way. But that in itself poses a problem. While from the outset I have sought to make this a listening book, the fact remains that it is a book, not a conversation. How do we listen to voices on a page? You will probably be reading this book alone, silently, inside your own head. It is likely that should you finish it, you will not read it a second time but put it on a shelf, pass it on or discard it. That is what we tend to do with the written word in our own age. Words expressing human thought have become part of the disposable, or even recycling, culture we have created. In that sense, while the words I am writing on this page might be read by any number of people I am never likely to meet, there is also something impersonal about them. As we read them to ourselves they have no sound and so we are robbed of something vital. This was not always so.

Before the arrival of the printing press, in the days when manuscripts were painstakingly reproduced by hand, those who read did so out loud to others. The scriptures in particular were heard rather than read in silence. Those who have read aloud to public gatherings will know that words read in this way have a different feel to them from when we read them silently in our heads. Sometimes we find something new in what was a quite familiar text. I find this particularly so when reading the Gospels, knowing that much of these texts probably existed only in spoken story form for several decades.

This was the power of the parables and their genius is the oblique way in which they come at the truth. They are particularly useful in getting past the defences of those who are so familiar with them that they feel superior to them.[2] The synoptic authors agree the first parable to be that of the sower and the four soils, which is a parable about hearing. It is the overture parable to all that Jesus teaches in the Gospels. It should not be reduced to something that we read silently in a book, for it is intended for the ear. Whoever has ears to hear, then hear!

> Jesus is speaking the seed words of God into our ears: pavement ears in which no seed can germinate, rocky ears in which no seed can sink roots, weedy ears in which no seed can mature, and good soil ears in which all seed bears fruit. The greatest thing going on in this history, in this earth is that God is speaking. The dominical command is *Listen*.[3]

However, as with scripture, listening to the written word presupposes that it be read. We have to read before we can listen, but we need to acknowledge that we can also read without going on to listen: a case of in one ear and out the other. In the fourth Gospel particularly, Jesus is described as the Word, and as the Word he brings the men and women of that gospel into conversation with God. Jesus spends a good deal of time challenging those readers of scripture who have lost the art of listening to God speaking through scripture – if they ever had it at all.

> You have never heard his voice or seen his form, and you do not have his word abiding in you, because you do not believe in him whom he has sent.

You search the scriptures because you think that in them you have eternal life; and it is they that testify on my behalf. Yet you refuse to come to me to have life.

John 5.37–40

Instead, he insists that the word always exists first and foremost as sound, to be heard and listened to. It is likely that the Johannine church expressed itself in this way when it met. Everything they read became alive because they listened. The departed Jesus lived for them through their voices.

I don't want to accord what I am writing here the status of holy scripture, but it does seem to me that we can learn something important from the way these early Christians understood what they meant by Christ among them, teaching radical and, to the establishment, unacceptable interpretations of scripture and life. Listening as fasting might be one way of hearing the voices we have pledged to listen to, and perhaps listening to the sound of the voices on the page might be another. It need not be in a public place, just in one that enables us to hear the sound of those voices through our ears, rather than silently in our heads. Try it!

The bishops and primates meeting as a result of the 1998 Lambeth Conference discovered two important things. We have already noted the first, that they could not reach a common mind regarding a single pattern for holy living for homosexual people, and we have also noted no real surprise in that discovery. As we have seen, in matters demanding pronouncement from above in the Church there is such a high degree of difference between the bishops themselves that it is often impossible for them as a collective to agree and deliver other than in compromise. Furthermore, given the degree of difference among themselves (they were an international group representing diverse cultures with different perceptions of homosexuality), what kind of uniform pattern could they offer for gay and lesbian couples in over 150 member countries of the Anglican Communion? The second thing the bishops discovered was that when they met together and adopted the ascetic of listening in silence they found a deeper meeting point than in the debating hall of the conference. They made progress when they met face to face.

The numerous interviews that have formed the basis of this book have been an endorsement of this insight. Meeting couples face to face, sometimes in the homes they shared, was both very ordinary and very moving. For some the simple activity of living side by side was risking the very thing that most of us normally take for granted. Theirs are the voices on the pages of this book, but the written word is no substitute for this kind of personal encounter, encounters that allowed hospitality to be offered and received in the food that we shared and then in the stories that emerged.

The bishops and primates could not offer a single pattern for holy living because there probably isn't one, either for gays and lesbians or anyone else. This, too, ought not to be a surprise. We live in an age of religious pluralism and most of the time we acknowledge that and accept it, allowing this context to challenge and shape us. Religious pluralism thus shakes complacency; through it we have to think more clearly about issues of faith and why particular things matter. Why then should it be any different when faced with the lives and needs of gay and lesbian couples? Why should not such relationships similarly challenge faith values and shake complacency? Far from berating such couples for living as they do, we owe them a phenomenal debt for the insights that they offer to the rest of the Body of Christ.

I reminded each couple of the stalemate conclusion drawn by the working party of bishops and primates, and asked them what they had learned from life together in partnership and community, about trying to live patterns of Christian holiness. What, if they could speak to this working party face to face, might they say to them?

Holy living – hope for the future and waiting on God

What emerged was a sequence of virtues and qualities that under-pinned life in a Church context that they continued to commit them-selves to. What held them within that multifarious context was a continued sense of hope for a better future. This sense of hope was a key virtue of holy living. The commitment to serving God openly and honestly sustained the couples when they were at their lowest ebb. Hope for the future was not simply about being in partnership with one another, but being in partnership with the whole Body of Christ and particularly with those instrumental in leading the Church. Many continued to hope for a listening partnership that might lead to better understanding and acceptance of who they were and how they lived.

I think that the notion of the bishops and primates coming up with some sort of code for people in partnership like me might be helpful and I would not be unhappy with that. It seems to me that if they are willing to listen to the likes of me and everyone else that you have interviewed they might see for themselves how God can work through a partnership like ours in the same way as God might work through a married couple. I really want them to know how God has blessed and enabled me and that this is about serving God together. I want them to know that this is absolutely happening for me.

Female ordinand with partner 3 years

Hope for the future was joined by the need to watch and wait. Waiting can be interpreted as a rather benign, passive activity. The call for reflection by the Church on the issue of same-sex partnerships seems to have been in some cases little more than a stalling activity in which any real self-searching has been postponed. This is not in keeping with the cultivation of holy living in which the ability to wait involves a real sense of resilience. Keeping vigil is a purposeful exercise and, for the couples, living a holy life requires a commitment and a high degree of application, particularly when it feels that the Church is conspiring against them. Many said that it was an uphill struggle to live honestly in a Church context that seemed to be complicit with secrecy and punitive of openness.

I think that both of us feel that we have a lot to say about how much this way of life has cost us in terms of personal integrity. Honesty and truthfulness have to be put on one side in a context where we are required to be dishonest and dis-integrated – the very things we prized most highly.

Female ordinand with partner 4 years

By the same token, when they stood back from the pressures of living in secret, they deemed it remarkable that gay and lesbian people were still prepared to respond to the call of God to serve as clergy in the Church. At his consecration in New Hampshire, Gene Robinson reminded those gathered that although much of the focus of the consecration had been on him and the way he conducted his life by living openly with a partner of the same sex, the event was not really about him. It was about God and an unveiling or revealing of God at work in human life.

> This occasion is not about me, but a God who loves us beyond our wildest imagination. It is about so many other people who find themselves at the margins ... he is a God of unimaginable compassion and love.[4]

Thus the call to holy living was a call to discern the activity of God in their daily living. By their fruit shall you know them. There was a similar sense in which couples, faced with the pressure to leave the Church (as some have) or knuckle down quietly and not rock the boat (although some do), were aware of God's grace at work. It was an extraordinary thing that had sustained them; and not only sustained, but enabled them to flourish, in their calling to ministry as priests.

> *I agree with her and now that I feel that we have been cornered into living in this way and having to try and make some sense of the whole damn thing I think it is extraordinary that God continues to call gay people to serve the Church in this way and to live in partnership with others of the same sex and continue to serve. I think that it is even more extraordinary that people like her continue to respond.*
>
> *Partner of 4 years to female ordinand*

Holy living: a challenge to the Church

Holy living is a challenging way of life. If it is the mission of the Church to capture the imagination of wider society in our age then this challenge has to be open. Another idea that emerged was the sense that holy living and committed partnership might be an activity in which God disturbs the Church. Many couples emerging from the complicity of imposed celibacy or fearful loneliness felt liberated. They were discovering themselves as human beings with the capacity to share intimately and faithfully. They then discerned this as a challenge, not only to themselves and their own longing to live openly, but to those parts of the Church that were still unable to accept not only that they might exist at all but live in this way. In turn this begged the question of how, in the search for holy living within the Body of Christ, they could fulfil that in a creative way, that didn't present itself as a kind of retaliation for the rejection they had experienced from various parts of the Church, including senior pastors. Clearly many had felt hurt and rejected.

Publicly what Lambeth has told me is that my life is incompatible with the life of a priest.

Male priest with partner 20 years

I get cross by what is called the gay lifestyle. When I look at what my life is, it is exactly the same as everyone else's . . . It is just ordinary. It is no different from the couple who live next door . . .

Male priest with partner 20 years

They make all these declarations about listening and learning and it never seems to be followed through.

Male partner to priest 20 years

I wish we could talk to them about our real life so that they could see how dull and how boring most of it is. It might make the whole thing seem less exotic in their minds and they could get more real about it.

Male priest with partner 15 years

Holy living: community and holy ground

The call to holy living was also the call to hospitality. Several clergy wished that they could share openly with their senior pastors who they were and how being a couple had sustained them in ministry together. Most had not been able to do this, as the warning signs had been clear. But others had tried and been ignored. One priest broke down as he relayed how his longing to be acknowledged had been studiously unacknowledged by his senior pastor.

> *I would say to the bishops and primates, talk to us and pastor us. If they just come and have a meal with us, just acknowledge that we're here . . . they are meant to be our pastors.*
>
> *Male priest with partner 7 years*

For others, being unacknowledged simply left them in a place of isolation. There were times when this could be a lonely and dark place, but some declared that they emerged from it with their faith strengthened. Being uncertain as to where they stood in relation to other parts of the Body of Christ, who were clearly uncertain about them, led them to test the sense of blessing they felt in the life of another with whom they had come to share in a deep and intimate way.

> *Having come out, and having been an evangelical, I wrote to a friend who worked for Scripture Union hoping for his support and possibly even approval. I was trying to tell him that I realized that I was gay but had come to feel that it might be possible that this was a God-given part of my whole self and I wanted him to understand that. He simply said nothing and left me wondering where I stood. I resolved then that what I would do would be to try to live out my life as a life of faith under the guidance of God's Spirit. What I have come to find is that the more I have depended on God in this way, the more confident I became of God's blessing on me as a gay Christian man.*
>
> *Male ordinand with partner 7 years*

The call to hospitable holy living is not exclusive to the Church. As a parish priest I find this time and again, beyond the life of the congregation in the wider parish community. The most obvious example is in the visits I make to families preparing for the funeral of someone they cared deeply about. Most of the time, at that visit and at the funeral service, I will be the only person present who did not know the deceased. Yet they will want me to speak as though I did. To that end they open up their home, their photograph album and their family history to me, a stranger in their midst. We talk, face to face. It may be difficult at first, but it does not seem a strange thing to do, and generally we all feel better for it afterwards. Even if we never spend such time together again, the welcome they have offered and the hospitality they have shared becomes the springboard for a new perspective of life together in the local community. We simply see each other in a different way. That is the grace of the gift of hospitality. It is open and it strengthens our understanding of community. So why not apply the same insight to the very couples that appear to be the cause of such concern?

> In the search for holy living we have discovered that we are stronger together than we would be apart. We are more faithful to God's calling together than we would be apart. Our house is an open house where we welcome people and it would be so nice if we were to be in a situation that was both acknowledged and was publicly open so that they could see that what exists here is real.
>
> Female priest with partner 2 years

In his book *Reaching Out*, Henri Nouwen describes an encounter with a former student who has returned to the campus and seeks him out for apparently no reason whatever.[5] The young man arrives declaring that he wants nothing from his former teacher other than to celebrate some time with him. The two begin to talk effusively about the past and what they have been doing since they last met before eventually falling silent. The silence, Nouwen tells us, is not an uncomfortable one punctuated by small talk or needing to be filled with clever words. Instead, it is a silence that enables them to realize something deep and positive between them, and they tell each other how good it is to be in touch again. Then the former student makes the startling remark that when he looks at Nouwen it is as if he is in the presence of Christ. He goes on to amaze his former teacher by declaring that from that moment onwards, wherever the two of them travelled, all the ground between them would be holy ground.

It is from the place of hospitality that our sense of community begins to grow. Through our commitment to holy living, all the ground between us becomes holy ground. For the Body of Christ, pledged to listen to its gay and lesbian members (including its clergy), this has to be a prerequisite for being part of the Body at all. If out of the place of isolation something creative can emerge, this will only happen if we make some silent space in which it can be received. Some couples found that because they were forced to hide their relationships, they had to work harder at them, often pioneering new ways of expressing faithfulness and commitment that because they went unnoticed also went unapplauded.

I suppose the other thing that I would say about the fact that we don't have blessings and that we don't have models that we can take off the shelf and say look, here is an authentic way of doing it, the fact that we have to struggle our way through, I wish people could see the goodness that has come from it through sheer effort.

Male priest with partner 15 years

The creation of the silent space might allow these unnoticed ways of life to be noted, and perhaps applauded too.

Holy living as repentance and forgiveness

Noticing things in each other can bring the opportunity for change. This can only occur with the right kind of listening. The other day I found myself deploying the wrong kind of listening when I was accosted in the churchyard of a neighbouring parish church. The young man, who assumed I was the parish priest, berated me for the state of the churchyard (which was actually in quite good order!) and proceeded to hurl a torrent of what seemed to me to be abuse.

I needed to return to the values of the New Testament church, he screamed. There was a straight choice come judgement day, it was either heaven or hell. I was having a bad day, and he had caught me unexpectedly. The vehemence of his anger combined with the volume with which he dispelled it in this public place made my hackles rise. He made me very angry and I stopped listening to him. Instead I became defensive, trying to beat him at his own game and outbox him with words, while making my way to the exit. It must have looked a ridiculous scene to the office workers on the churchyard benches eating their lunches in the sunshine.

I have been thinking about this incident for some days. I am no longer hooked by his anger, but am disappointed that I didn't hear it for what it was at the time. I can easily dismiss his actions as those of one who was clearly unbalanced, but that is really beside the point. I stopped listening, and the opportunity to do anything other than reject him was lost.

It would seem that the angry exchange which has hitherto dominated the discourse in the Church on gay and lesbian relationships has gone this way too. There has been a lot of angry shouting, resulting in the ultimate rejection of opinion, position and person. Individuals and entire church communities have become defensive and entrenched, filling the empty space with the sound of their own voices. Some have declared their pulpits off-limits to any who cannot subscribe to their received policy on homosexuals. Some even require their bishop to make a statement of affirmation on the Lambeth resolution before allowing them to lead worship at their church. This is hardly a template for holy living in the Body of Christ, through which we should be committed to the noticing in each other, through listening to each other, the kind of things that might elicit change for the good of all. Christian defensiveness that masks itself as the protection of orthodoxy is an ugly vandalism of the Body. Its hallmarks are found in unpleasant name-calling, paranoia over alleged agendas, in threats to declare UDI or to replace a bishop if the one we have doesn't think the same way that we do.

The phrase 'call to repentance' is one that my young man in the churchyard might have bandied at me, although he did not. It is a phrase that makes me squirm with embarrassment when I hear Christians drop it into everyday conversation. It has become synonymous with sin and narrow in its deployment. However, it would appear that Christians borrowed it from Plato, who used the term to mean having a change of mind or purpose on anything.[6] So anyone who has thought about an issue and had a change of heart or mind has made an act of repentance, or perhaps more accurately, committed themselves to a process of repentance. It might be associated with a sin, something that deflects the disciple's vision of God, but often it might not. I am not sure if my encounter with the angry young man in the churchyard was inherently sinful, but it was certainly something that has, in this sense, made me feel repentant. I find this broader reading of the term repentance much more helpful than the narrower definition that seems to be the personal possession of a religious few. Perhaps it is time to restore it in its broadest sense to the entire Body of Christ, for the benefit of the whole Body? Furthermore, to see repentance as a process that the whole Church is committed to participating in would give a much healthier view of the Church for it would encourage precisely the kind of listening I am advocating. It is no good telling gays and lesbians to repent of their relationships, when the activity of repentance might actually mean change for us all, a change in which we all learn to listen better and perhaps even come to view relationships under God differently from before.

Similar things might also apply to forgiveness. Although liturgically forgiveness and absolution exist in the form of a pronouncement, the realization of forgiveness, in both its giving and its receiving, can only be achieved in the working out of human relationships. Repentance involves a change of mind or heart and can be accorded to anyone; true forgiveness can also only come about in its fullest form if there has been a change of heart. That change of heart might exist equally for the forgiver as for the one forgiven. It has become too easy for people in the discussion on same-sex relations to see themselves as the victim, who might dispense forgiveness if the narrowest kind of repentance is offered. That is no forgiveness at all. As James Alison makes clear, it neatly avoids the responsibility for every Christian to understand themselves as *already* forgiven, and for that reason

FACE TO FACE

capable of being a forgiving victim for another. Without it, we will never understand the salvation, which we are receiving from Christ.[7] That would be a travesty. One priest observed:

> Forgiveness and reconciliation are the most important things Christianity has to stress in relationships, but I am not sure what more the bishops could offer except to face the facts that people are gay and need to live that out. What I do expresses who I am. Simply to say that it is okay to be gay but not do anything about it makes a nonsense of the way we understand incarnation, the way God is and revealed.

> *Male priest with partner 2 years*

He is saying something very useful here. Just as a more active understanding of the doctrine of salvation might help us see ourselves as part of the healing process that God begins in us and which Christ exemplifies, a similar understanding of the doctrine of creation might enable a different interpretation of the salvific activity of Christ in redeeming that creation. What I think he means is this. As human beings we are the pinnacles of God's creation. Created is what we *are*; just as forgiven is what we *are*. It is a state of being rather than something we acquire. It is as created beings that we enter into relationship with God and that relationship is defined by how we behave towards one another as human beings. What we are is expressed in what we *do*. The things we do become the signs of God's creative, forgiving nature in the world. They express what God *is*. This applies to any of us, irrespective of our sexual inclinations. If the things we do are predatory, exploitative and destructive, they are clearly unredeemed expressions in need of penitent change. They do not show us God as love active in the world. But what this priest is implicitly saying is that if they are potentially enhancing, life-giving signs in which couples reflect the forgiven, created beings that we already are because of the salvation offered through Christ, it is not a question of whether gay men and lesbian women express their relationships or not. Instead it is *how* that relationship is expressed and whether, by the fruit of that expression, the nature of God in Christ is revealed. Is this a relationship of love, joy, peace? All expressions of God's creative forgiveness

185

need to be *seen* in individual lives to benefit the life of the whole Body of Christ. The call to holy living is the call to active forgiveness and reconciliation. It is what the Body of Christ is called to be, not simply what it tries to do.

Holy living: growing to mature personhood

The life of holiness is nothing if it is not about growing to full maturity. This understanding has been part of the Christian perspective since the foundation of the earliest Pauline churches. The Corinthians, we are told, are to be fed with milk and not solid food, because Paul deems them spiritually to be infants, squabbling among themselves and in disarray (1 Corinthians 3). However, to grow in holiness is *to grow*, and this seems to be a principal concern of the apostle as he cares for the young and rather difficult church in Corinth.

Taking responsibility in life is not the same as doing our own thing. The tendency in recent years has been towards a culture of individualism in Western Europe and North America. It found expression in the psychological language that emerged from California in the 1960s and 1970s: the ethos that determined that you do your thing and I do mine and we are not responsible for each other's decisions. The legacy of this can be seen in the political ideology in the 1990s which seeks the demolition of social responsibility, including the infamous declaration that there is no such thing as society, only individuals.

The Church too, and the world of Practical Theology (the discipline through which theological insight is discovered in practice), found itself caught in this phenomenal cultural revolution, quite unable to keep pace with it. In the same era, Pastoral and Practical Theology, once defined by Schleiermacher as 'the crown of theological studies', suffered a similar identity crisis and took on a Cinderella status. It then became engulfed by the eruption of the pastoral counselling movement.

Clearly some good things did emerge from this period, and the taking of responsibility for oneself and one's actions was an example. However, the elevation of the individual with scant regard for society and the building of community is clearly contrary to those values of the Kingdom explored in earlier chapters. So how do we combine the two?

It is completely ludicrous to be thinking about waiting around for the digni-taries of the Lambeth Conference every ten years to give anybody directives on how to live. It is important for gay and lesbian people to reflect on their lives for themselves, to talk openly about issues of love and passion and falling in love and commitment. I often think that we preoccupy ourselves with talking about same-sex ceremonies, but no one talks about commitment. For gay and lesbian people this is a big issue. How do you find a partner? How do you make a relationship? Do you aspire to a type of monogamy that is the received understanding of what is right? We need to do a lot more of that for ourselves.

Male priest with partner 4 years

The virtue of holy living expressed here is one in which this man and his partner describe the need to take responsibility for personal growth. If the creative forgiving activity of God is working itself out in the everyday events of life, then he is right. We all have the responsi-bility to develop creative insights that enhance our understanding of God at work. He is also right that the preoccupation with ceremonies of blessing have revealed issues of power and control in our religious institutions and masked the very thing that prompts them, which is the search for commitment. If the worldwide Church cannot create a safe place for that search then clergy and lay couples, since they are clearly not going to disappear, are going to be forced to get on with it alone.

This will be detrimental to our corporate understanding of holy living, because it will not enable the whole Body to benefit from the insights gained by these searches for commitment. Nor will the couples receive the kind of monitoring, feedback and support that should be the automatic requirement of living in the Body. There will be no open partnership.

Instead, the culture of 'you do your thing and I'll do mine' will prevail, as it already does in an institution that sees a great many of its members quite happy to go on pretending that gay and lesbian people, ordained and lay, don't exist, or if they do, not round here. It will be further detrimental in that it will allow the shrill voices, calling for punitive action under the sanitized umbrella of Church discipline and what they declare to be orthodoxy, to shout all other voices down.

Creating the right environment for personal growth to happen has been seen as an essential prerequisite. As long ago as 1988, the unpublished but widely leaked Gloucester report stated:

No serious work on moral growth can be achieved in an atmosphere marked by a judgemental and fearful spirit. When people think that they have nothing to learn and that their duty is to make others conform to their views, it is very difficult for growth to happen.

And in 1995 the late Michael Vasey was suggesting a way forward.

The first lies in personal encounter and dialogue – getting to know the gay people within and outside its life, and becoming involved with gay groups within the community. The second way is to take steps to defend the humanity of gay people, to acknowledge that they are part of the community, to examine and act on questions of social justice, to work with gay people in examining the results of stress, isolation and misrepresentation.[8]

However this great and obvious work takes place, it will not begin until it is owned as the responsibility of the whole Body. In that sense it is ludicrous to sit around and wait for the dignitaries of the Lambeth Conference to make recommendations, which then achieve the status of pronouncements on how to live. It is also irresponsible, for it is futile for the Lambeth bishops or anyone else to think that we really can live in isolation from one another. We each have to begin at the beginning and follow through to the end, knowing that all our starting points will be different. We need to ask, as we did in the earlier chapters of this book, where the signs of God's Kingdom are to be found in our human relationships within our own communities. We all have to do this in our own individual way.

The culture conditions us to approach people and situations as journalists: see the big, exploit the crisis, edit and abridge the commonplace, interview the glamorous. But the scriptures and our best pastoral traditions train us in a different approach: notice the small, persevere in the commonplace, appreciate the obscure.[9]

Where there is love there is God . . . so while living a life of Christian holiness may be difficult to quantify, those who want to make pronouncements or recommendations on what constitutes holy living really do need to go and see people's lives in action. It's the meeting face to face that really is transforming of opinions and attitudes.

Male priest with partner 32 years

Notes

1 Margaret R. Miles, *The Image and Practice of Holiness*, SCM Press, 1988, p. 104.
2 Eugene H. Peterson, *Working the Angles – The Shape of Pastoral Integrity*, Eerdmans, 2002, p. 104.
3 *Working the Angles*, p. 104.
4 *Guardian*, 3 November 2003.
5 Henri Nouwen, *Reaching Out – The Three Movements of the Spiritual Life*, Zondervan, 1998.
6 Malcolm Torry, *The Parish*, Canterbury Press, 2004, p. 165.
7 James Alison, *On Being Liked*, Darton, Longman and Todd, 2003, p. 38.
8 Michael Vasey, *Strangers and Friends*, Hodder and Stoughton, 1995, p. 210.
9 *Working the Angles*, p. 149.